MEDITATE

Breathe into meditation and awaken your potential

TALWINDER SIDHU

Disclaimer

The information provided in this book is designed to provide helpful information and support on the subjects discussed. This book is not meant to be used, nor should it be used, to diagnose or treat any mental illness or medical condition. For diagnosis or treatment of any medical problem or mental health issue, consult a physician and/or a mental health professional.

The publisher and author are not responsible for any specific health or mental health needs that may require medical supervision, and are not liable for any damages or negative consequences from any treatment, action, application, or preparation, to any person reading or following the information in this book.

References are provided for informational purposes only and do not constitute endorsement of any websites or other sources. Readers should be aware that the websites listed in this book may change. If you are affected by any of the topics discussed in this book, particularly suicide, please call your local suicide hotline number and talk to someone. Please visit: http://www.suicide.org/international-suicide-hotlines.html to locate a hotline number near you.

ISBN: 978-1-7772869-0-3

Edited by: Katie Chambers, Beacon Point LL

Cover Design & Formatting: Ida Fia Sveningsson

'Ik Onkar, Sat-naam'

— Guru Nanak

There is only one source of creation;
its name is Truth.

DOWNLOAD YOUR FREE
MEDITATION STARTER PACK

READ THIS FIRST

Learning to meditate will take practise and to help you
get started quickly, I have compiled a meditation starter pack
which you can download for free by visiting

www.meditatethebook.com/starterpack

THE PACK INCLUDES:

An Introduction to meditation (excerpt from this book)
A quick guide video on the five-step process
A quick start guided meditation audio

TABLE OF CONTENTS

MY MEDITATION JOURNEY

I grew up in a large family, and every weekend, it seemed we had another function to attend at someone's house. Engagements, birthdays, religious and cultural gatherings, new jobs, new cars, new houses, getting out of the hospital, out of jail, graduations, and so on. If there was a reason to celebrate, there was a reason to gather.

The events would always unfold the same way: the men would eat and drink in one room, the women would cook and serve from another, and the kids would separate in their collective age groups and keep themselves entertained. It seemed to work for everyone but myself because I did not know where I was supposed to be. I did not really fit in, so I would just wander from room to room until the men were ready to leave.

I was a quiet kid so I would often go unnoticed. I could sneak into any place and eavesdrop on any conversation and learn of the goings-on that were happening behind closed doors. On the surface, the women always seemed happy, but beneath their smiles were conversations of abuse, fear, and sadness.

The men would drink, eat, and relax from a hard day's labour and exchange stories of what life was like back in India. They would discuss their challenges of life in England and engage in political debates that I could never understand. Then as the food went cold and the alcohol neared the bottom of the bottle, I would witness tears and fragility followed by anger and occasionally fighting, which scared me.

The older kids were always paranoid when I was about because they did not want me to listen in on what they were up to, in fear of me telling on them. The kids my age would only let me hang out with them if they needed an extra person to even the teams for games; otherwise, just like at school, I'd be sitting on the sidelines wondering what was wrong with me. I really had nothing else to do but wander around the house and observe.

When I was around nine years old, my mother taught me yoga and meditation to help me cope with bullying and the stresses of growing up poor in a working-class environment in the West Midlands region of England. By age twelve I was meditating independently and started developing my own meditation techniques. I soon could recognise the elusive nature of reality by reading translated passages of Hindu and Sikh scriptures, and I started studying the landscape of what it meant to be human.

Meditation was an instrumental tool that enabled me to develop independence within my own mind. It helped me cope with the isolation of feeling alone and like an outsider among my peers. Growing up in a Sikh community, meditation was a religious practice and the resources I was often drawn to were that of a religious and philosophical nature. Yet because these topics weren't exactly conversations cool kids wanted to discuss, I feared ridicule at school if I started talking about the notion of God and the state of creation, so I would sit silently in meditation to explore my notions freely within my own mind. I didn't even tell anyone I meditated, only my mum knew. I was already too weird among my peers at school and not man enough for the Punjabi community. I struggled to fit in already, so I didn't want to be seen as religious too.

In an immigrant community in the UK, I felt as if I lived in four worlds: a religious one, a Punjabi one, an Indian one, and an English one. The conversations I wanted were only being discussed in the religious one, but the demands of the life of a working-class family in the UK meant less and less time at the temple. Through meditation, I learned that I could be anyone I chose to be. I felt that my identity was merely an expression of my inner truths and that the only experience of life that mattered was whatever was going on in life at present.

What I had eaten for breakfast to how I was beaten up at school were just experiences to learn from and not experiences to hold onto, for they had already expired and no longer existed, though I struggled with developing a sense of identity because of the lack of alternative narratives available for me to express and comprehend who I was.

By the time I was sixteen, I had learned how to navigate through this experience called life. I learned to be smart and stay out of trouble by playing ignorant, and I began mimicking the behaviours of the men around me. As life started to ease up, I began getting popular at school and became interested in psychology and human behaviour. Since meditation had been my way of coping, I figured I no longer needed that tool to survive. I never grasped how it could help me understand other people beyond deciphering those who lived life in conflict and those who did not. I suppose I lacked the context to help me understand human motivation and the things I felt were true about people. I felt meditation was not going to serve me much further than developing the creative imagination I once needed to cope in a life without friends, and I needed to study people to understand people.

Also, post-puberty, my motivations in life rapidly changed, as my body wanted to play in different ways and life responded to me in different ways too.

I figured I did not require meditation as a tool to survive and started neglecting my practice. A decision I would later regret.

By the age of eighteen, I had started to formally study psychology. I became fascinated by behavioural and psychodynamic psychology, and I truly grasped an understanding of how humans learned and learned to live. However, I could not understand why after two years of study, there was no mention of meditation as a way to restore mental health, improve cognitive function, and expand conscious awareness.

I had learned a lot about medication, on the other hand. Which to me did not seem to make much sense. Why would you medicate someone before teaching them how to meditate? I thought patients should at least learn how to assess the validity of their own reality for themselves before diagnosing them with a definitive disorder. The mind operates differently than the body and it seemed what I was learning was counterintuitive to developing a healthy mind. Although I do believe psychology provides a lot of practical applications, such as EMDR (Eye Movement Desensitization and Reprocessing) as a tool to combat post-traumatic stress disorder (PTSD), it is a shame that only a privileged few can access or know how to access such services.

I moved to Canada soon after university and started a life coaching practice at the age of twenty-five. Around the same time, I started meditating again.

LIFE COACHING TO MEDITATION COACHING

After a failed interview where the interviewer suggested I become a life coach, I looked into it and found that the program was developed by psychologists, and they were missing components such as meditation, planning for contingencies, and how to sustain personal development independently. Already in debt and not wanting to invest in a program that I had already found a few holes in, I figured I would develop my own comprehensive life planning tool and go rogue.

Despite not having any formal life coach training and being one of the youngest professional life coaches in the industry, I quickly became sought after for my unique approach to personal development and my mental health services. I had never intended to support individuals through mental health disorders. I had become a life coach because I wanted to motivate and inspire people to live the lives they wanted.

On my website, I had written that I teach meditation to help my clients stay focused on their personal development and to stay productive. I was only teaching what I thought were basic instructions that I had learned from my mother growing up and a few techniques I had developed from my own personal practice. And I viewed it as just one tool in the toolbox, but the more I taught it, the more people reached out for support with their mental health disorders.

Normally, I would have to refer such people to psychiatrists and counsellors but the opposite was happening: mental health professionals were referring their clients to my practice because of a small sentence that had climbed the search engine ranks in Vancouver: 'I teach my clients how to meditate'. I soon became inundated with requests for consultations.

All was going swimmingly until 2018 when I burned out and was ready to give up on my coaching practice, struggling to keep up with the demand. I was struggling with having so many clients dealing with anxiety, depression, and an overwhelming desire to give up on their lives. A third of the people I was helping could not afford my services, but I could not say no and helped them for free. I feared what these people may do to themselves if I had turned them away. My parents never turned away a person in need and their example became my way of operating too.

Yet working twelve- to fourteen-hour days, seven days a week, was hurting my well-being and I too was starting to develop anxiety and hatred for my life. I was meditating less and working around the clock. I was losing sleep and money as I struggled to cope with running a business and being there for my clients. Part of what made my service unique was the email and text support I provided throughout the program, but I just couldn't keep up. Feeling overwhelmed by coaching, I figured I would learn how to teach meditation from some local yoga teachers in Vancouver, get qualified, and begin teaching meditation more and scale back my life coaching services.

As I researched various meditation programs and spoke to local teachers, I discovered that meditation was not being taught as comprehensively as yoga. Nobody seemed to be teaching people how to meditate beyond offering stress-reducing techniques like mindfulness and gimmicky guided meditations.

Where were the tools which released fear and gave someone command of their human experience? Where were the techniques which helped people detach from trauma and personal revelations? Where were the teachings which inspired people to seek enlightenment? So much knowledge was missing, the knowledge that taught people how to independently transform their experience of life and take ownership of their bodies.

By the summer of 2018, I made the conscious decision to begin formally teaching my homegrown meditation practice, and a year later, I was teaching meditation full-time. I was confidently helping people who struggled with addiction, childhood trauma, learning difficulties, anxiety disorder, and depression. I was also able to teach meditation in groups which made my services more accessible and helped ease the demand for life coaching.

I also began teaching cannabis-friendly meditation techniques to support medicinal-cannabis patients to better manage their psychoactive states. I also provided services in support of psychedelic harm reduction too. The meditation effect was remarkable, people were very responsive, the class would engage openly in philosophical discussion, and I was moved by the appreciation people shared. I realised I had something to offer that people genuinely needed, so I moved my life coaching practice online and relocated to Nelson, BC, to open a boutique meditation studio.

Within my first month of opening, I was already teaching meditation in schools to children as young as five years old and to seniors in the community as old as ninety-five. No matter the age, gender, socioeconomic status, or cultural background, we always had an enlightening discussion about life, death, and creation. All this goes to show how effective meditation is, how simple it is, and how it brings people together.

My classes always brought together an eclectic mix of people, and it was wonderful to see them all getting on and engaging in dialogue about mental health and personal experiences. It was healing for me, I felt a lot of hope and admiration for this world, which, if I am being honest, was something I was starting to struggle with after hearing so many stories about trauma and abuse.

I found it easier to teach meditation than I did life coaching. It was also more accessible to people than coaching was. Where life coaching requires a lot of one-on-one time, I could teach meditation to a whole class and help more people in one go. I now only take a handful of new life coaching clients a year, focusing most of my efforts on teaching meditation full time, as I'm keen to develop new practices to support those with mental health issues and learning difficulties.

When COVID hit, I had extra time on my hands in isolation, so I decided to write this book. I figured if I came here to teach meditation, then that is what I must do in one way or another. Teaching meditation is my truth, and it's been part of my life since I can remember. I feel that every challenge and direction in my life led me here to this point today. I feel that life is a divine orchestration and the only thing I did was listen.

INTRODUCTION

THE STATE OF MENTAL HEALTH

As I write this book, the world has come to a standstill. The global coronavirus pandemic has forced us into isolation and has distanced us from our communities. Social distancing measures have had a severe impact on the way we navigate through the world, seek support, and connect with our loved ones. A viewpoint published by the American Medical Association, 'Suicide Mortality and Coronavirus Disease 2019', suggests that the world will see an increase of mental health disorders and suicides as a consequence of social distancing and the financial crisis that is expected to follow.

The World Health Organization (WHO) already estimates that one in every ten people has lived with a mental health disorder, such as depression, anxiety disorders, eating disorders, or addictions. That is at least 10 percent of the world's population and these numbers only reflect reported cases. According to the WHO, 'most mental health disorders remain widely under-reported' and research continues to show increasing trends.

The WHO also reports that over 800,000 people are taking their own lives every year, and for each suicide, there are more than twenty suicide attempts. This means that if each one of those attempted suicides was successful, the global figure would climb up to 16,000,000. The state of the world's mental health is in crisis and more needs to be done to fight this global pandemic. One such solution: the world can benefit from learning how to meditate.

Over the past forty years, promising psychological studies are showing how meditation can support an individual's mental health and improve their overall well-being. A paper written by Dr Jooyoung Julia Shin, MD, 'The Physiology of Meditation', outlines a variety of research that demonstrates the incredible mental and physical health benefits of meditation. Shin's findings show how meditation enhances happiness, decreases anger, improves concentration, reduces anxiety, strengthens vitality, manages stress, supports the endocrine and central nervous systems, and increases creativity.

More recently, in 2015, a journal by Dr Hari Sharma, MD, 'Meditation: Process and effects', summarises research that confirms a myriad of physiological and psychological health benefits that are gained by meditating. Sharma's findings also show how meditation decreases anxiety and depression, reduces physical and psychological pain, improves memory and cognitive function, increases energy, and numerous other mental health benefits that can recover a person's joy and happiness. Put simply, regular meditation could save your life.

Over the last seven years, I have been teaching meditation as a way to help my life coaching clients reduce stress and stay focused on their goals.

WHAT YOU WILL LEARN

In this book, I will:

- Introduce you to what meditation is from an ancient Indian perspective.
- Teach you how to meditate with my five-step meditation process to help you better manage your mental health.
- Outline a simple way to deepen your meditation practice and raise consciousness.
- Talk about the concept of chakras, an ancient Indian practice of unlocking innate wisdom, as a form of personal and spiritual development which I refer to as integrative development.

Over half a billion people around the world are affected by mental health disorders and nearly a million people are taking their own lives each year; this is a troubling number that can easily come down if more people meditated. Meditation can save your life and so long as you can breathe, you can meditate. I promise you it is that simple.

SECTION I

INTRODUCTION TO MEDITATION

CHAPTER I
WHAT IS MEDITATION?

Meditation comes in many forms, but no matter which approach you adopt, you will soon realise that they all are trying to explain the same thing just in different ways.

Think of a problem that you are currently dealing with in your life today. Now think of the problem as a creation that has its own life separate from you. Now assess how the problem came into existence. How did your problem come to life? How was it created? This is the first basic principle I understood about meditation: to assess all experiences in life from the perspective of a creator so you can discover that experience's true origin.

Essentially, sitting in meditation is to study the origin of an experience of life—whether that experience is a sensation in your present, a memory from your past, or a state of mind that is directing your future. You can even study the origin of life itself and raise consciousness into realms beyond the experience of life altogether, and all this can be achieved by simply creating a moment for yourself and sitting in contemplation. Also known as meditation.

Sitting in meditation is to study experience, a creation, from the perspective of a creator. You are a creator, and if you struggle to meditate, it only means that you struggle to see yourself as one. Perhaps something else or someone else has taken charge of your life. Seeing yourself as a creator is how you are going to combat your mental ailments and effectively meditate. For instance, if a problem has been created in your life, then a solution can be created too.

When you learn how to observe everything that your mind presents as creation and learn to see everything in life as a creation, you will begin to effectively meditate and arrive at conclusions that can help you create a solution and evolve. For example, if anxiety is an experience that has been created in your life, then calmness is an experience that can be created too. If trauma has been created in your life, then healing can be created too. If addiction has been created in your life, then sovereignty can be created too.

You first need to learn how to detach from whatever experience you are consumed by so you can attain conscious control and reassert your presence. (You will learn how to do this in Section 2,

Beginning to Meditate.) Solving your life's problems and creating solutions is just the beginning of what meditation can help you achieve. Meditation can help you raise awareness beyond the experience of life itself, which can make whatever you are dealing with in life a minor inconvenience. (This will be explored in Section 3, Deepening Your Meditation.) Meditation also encourages you to pay attention to the innate intelligence within. Listening to your body and how it responds to and functions in life can really help you turn your life around. (This will be explored in the final sections of this book, Integrative Development.)

THE ORIGINS OF MEDITATION

The origins of meditation are as complex as the practice of meditation itself. The earliest mentions of meditation are found in the ancient Indian scriptures known as the Vedas. The Vedic scriptures date back to 1500 BCE, though their true origin date is unknown as the scriptures were traditionally passed down through generations orally, in the form of chants and hymns. What is fascinating about these scriptures is that the knowledge contained within these sacred texts are discoveries derived from meditations, conducted by ancient Indian sages known as the rishis.

The ancient rishis had deduced that everything in life must have derived from one singular source, such as how all the different species of plants in a forest can sprout from the same earth, and how the moon, stars, and all the planets floating in space can exist in the same universe. No matter how far you build something up or how small you break it down, everything comes together to form one construct or starts as one construct.

Where did all this creation begin and where does it end? To understand a rishi is to understand a spiritual scientist: How does one find the source of creation without tearing the creations of the world into pieces to look for the creator inside? Furthermore, even if such an approach were to be adopted, each tangible piece of creation that could be observed through the physical senses would only lead them back to the same conundrum: What is the source of this creation?

The rishis were smart enough to realise that there was nothing that they could experience through their physical senses, which would enable them to conclusively locate that source of creation, so they had to look beyond anything in life. The next logical place to look was inside the mind.

Your dreams are not physically experienced in life. Your memories are also experiences that no longer exist in life. Your thoughts and ideas too, though they can be brought into life, still very much start in your mind and not in your physical life. The rishis figured out that creation starts from within, quite literally too, when you think of a seed sprouting life and a mother giving birth. Life experienced with the body is a distinctly separate experience from life within your mind. In fact, the rishis understood that life is much more expansive within.

EXERCISE

Look at your hand and notice how it exists in life. Now close your eyes and visualise your hand. Notice how what you are seeing is not your physical hand; instead, you are looking at a memory of it. While in your mind, move your hand side to side. Now open your eyes and look at your hand again and move it side to side exactly as you did in your mind. Notice how you just had three very different experiences?

1. You saw your hand in life: your physical hand that is attached to your body in the present.

2. You saw your hand in a state after life: the memory of your hand was revived from the past, an experience you had in life.

3. You saw your hand in creation, a pre-life state: you predetermined an experience and created it in life. You essentially saw your hand in the future and brought the future to your present.

Your mental health works in a very similar way but, of course, with more attachment to the experience in mind. Reimagining your hand and moving it side to side is not as traumatic as, say, someone reimagining a car crash when they almost died and believing it is going to happen again. This is why you practise detachment in meditation first: you detach, witness the process of creation, and consciously change it and the response. Remember, you are the creator of your own experience of life.

The next job for the rishis was to understand what or who is having this experience in the mind, because the body is evidently on the outside and isn't existing within. What is this entity that is living in your body and having experiences in the present, travelling into the past to revive the experiences it once had and no longer exist in the present, and creating a future ahead of the present, bringing it to life?

This entity is what we would call consciousness, and the term carrying consciousness or raising consciousness is referring to its ability to travel or exist beyond the experience of present life. Evidently, consciousness can move through time but your body cannot; the body can only ever exist in the present moment. Therefore, the world within is already more expansive than the world that surrounds the body.

Already, just by using their minds, the rishis discovered that they could travel throughout time and beyond life. We exist as so much more than our bodies, so where else could consciousness go? How far can it travel? Also, what is the source of all these inner creations? The rishis set to work and began unlocking the secrets of the universe, and the Vedic hymns were born out of their meditations.

You can carry consciousness into realms of existence that the body simply cannot access, and this is the true power of meditation. Also, you could potentially carry consciousness down into other parts of your body. Imagine carrying consciousness into your blood cells and, perhaps, even into subatomic levels of existence to explore creation from the perspective of an atom. Imagine if you could consciously change how your cells behaved and alter your biological makeup. It may sound out of this world because technically, and theoretically, it is.

However, it is not completely out of the realm of possibility, especially when you start thinking about programming and brainwashing: how advertisements have the power to change how you think about yourself, how music can move you and your ability to love and empathise with others, and how energy and conscious signals can be exchanged. Consciousness can travel extensively, but you must open your mind and your heart in order to allow it, and meditating can help and teach you how.

Think about where you could carry consciousness if you were able to detach from all the experiences of your life and venture beyond all realms of time and space itself. Life is a mystery, but I am certain that the mystery is not going to be solved by stressing, creating conflict, and engaging in self-destructive behaviours. Just like our ancient ancestors seemed to have done, we will have a much greater chance of seeking answers from within by raising awareness above our inner dilemmas and seeking knowledge beyond life. Healing yourself is just the beginning.

From conscious awareness to conscious recovery to conscious travel, meditation can provide you with so much more than being able to clear away stress and restore your mental health. The intelligence you have access to is why meditation is so effective at reducing stress and combating mental illnesses. When you understand meditation well and what you can achieve by practising it, clearing the troubles within your mind can become quite a simple process.

You can potentially raise consciousness into such high states of awareness that your life's troubles and its difficulties can feel like mere inconveniences that you can choose to let go of. You may not be able to change your past experiences, but you can certainly let go of them and stop them from contaminating your present. Detachment (letting go) is what you will learn to exercise in the next section, where you will learn to take basic command of your life.

TYPES OF MEDITATION

You can meditate in several different ways; each way has a unique experience to offer. Perhaps you have heard of mindfulness, vipassana, or the transcendental styles of meditation popularised by western practices. Mindfulness meditation offers a state of mind and is excellent for recovery and stress reduction. Vipassana offers a state of being which enables you to accept things as they are.

Transcendental meditation offers inner peace and wellness, though traditionally speaking a meditation that has a transcendental effect technically provides a state of trance, sort of like deep states of REM sleep except you are conscious during the experience. One that I am looking forward to learning is the whirling meditation, the state of surrender and submission to a higher power—a technique derived from the Middle East and made famous by the Sufi poet, Rumi. Tantric meditation is a fan favourite which evokes the state of ecstasy and the union to a higher power through sexual exploration and sacred play.

There are as many ways to meditate as there are ways to exist and it's not always necessary to practise with any specific goal in mind. Every single person on this planet has something unique to provide. Every being contains a nugget of truth within them that they can bring into creation and enlighten the world with. The willingness to source your truth is how you raise consciousness and effectively meditate.

CHAPTER 2
THE MEDITATIVE MIND

The meditative mind is a fearless mind. It seeks the truth in everything. It is intelligent and mindful and compassionate and desires to understand. Where there is conflict, you can find clarity instead of chaos; where there is pain, you can find management instead of a response; and where there is ignorance, you could choose to seek knowledge and raise consciousness with meditation instead.

Your mind is like a conscious control centre that processes the data it has access to. This data is then processed into a reality which instructs you on what to do. The data your mind has access to is the information received from your physical senses (the present) and the knowledge it can retrieve from your memories (the past). The past and the present come together to formulate a new idea, a reality which instructs your direction (the future).

Your mind's job is to gather up this data and process it into an instruction that tells you what to do. From a meditative standpoint, your mind is where you determine what is real and what is not real.

Meditation allows you to harness control over the mind. It gives you the power to either accept or reject any experience of reality before you respond to it (e.g., anxiety, fear, paranoia), and with enough practise, meditation can put you in charge of the construction of your reality. Meditation places you in control of your experience of life.

Raising consciousness to this level of operation requires you to first train your mind:

1 At the beginning stages of your meditation practice, you are learning how to assert control over your mind and identify yourself as consciousness. To do this, you will be learning to prioritise and place your breath ahead of every sense, thought, and emotion to attain conscious control. As you practise and exercise control breathing, you will begin to disempower and alleviate symptoms of physical and emotional pain such as stress, anxiety, and depression.

2 Once you can assert control over your mind and how it responds to situations and circumstances, you will begin to raise self-awareness. Raising self-awareness is to be aware of your own presence in life and in your own mind. This will enable you to have better control over your behaviour and of your emotions. You will also learn to take more responsibility for yourself as you begin to recognise yourself as an independent conscious being.

3 As you exercise self-control, you will strengthen your meditation practice and can sit for longer periods with less distraction and more focus. Sitting for lengthier meditations is key to being able to process deeper-rooted personal issues and identify different realms of awareness. Now you can recognise the present, past, and future states of being, and start to develop a broader perspective of life and the world around you. I have noticed great improvements in clients who suffer from attention deficit disorder at this stage of practice.

4 A broader perspective of life can make you aware of how your mind functions and how you as an individual have learned to operate life and navigate through this world. This is when you will be able to forgive yourself for past mistakes, detach from deep-rooted traumas, slow down mental processes, and generally improve cognitive function. You will begin to recognise your innate intelligence. It is also at this stage when you will start to increase mindfulness and compassion.

5 As you realise how the mind works you can begin working to eliminate conscious contaminants such as trauma and fear. This will encourage you to lower defence mechanisms and release the guards which protect you in the present experience of life. As you become more present in life you will become more in tune with your body. You will begin to unlock your human potential and sense the power of your innate intelligence. You will recognise what you are capable of and begin to build an appreciation for your body.

6 This connection to your body will enable you to utilise your meditation to develop solutions to problems, especially where your health is concerned. You will also learn to listen to the innate wisdom contained within, developing self-trust and a self-actualised state of being. More on this can be found in the integrative development program in Section 4.

7 By this point, you are seeking only the truth. You are motivated to be the truest version of yourself and have the truest experience of life; therefore, you are primed and ready to raise consciousness into transcendence and this entire journey starts with breathing.

EXERCISE

Take a good look at everything around you, use all your senses to absorb your surroundings. . . . Now focus all of your attention on breathing while looking a second time. . . . Notice how breathing consciously places you in the scene that you are in, whereas prior to breathing consciously you were merely a part of the scene itself. You went from having a subjective experience of the world to an objective one.

Every time you breathe consciously with focus and control, you effectively create a distinction between yourself and your reality. Reality becomes this secondary experience separated by breath. It becomes primary when it is merged with the breath, a sort of conscious merger if you will. Liken your breath to a hook: if life is becoming too much to handle, just breathe consciously as if to unhook yourself from the moment to observe the experience, and when you feel calm and in control, breathe freely and remerge with life.

Exercising conscious breathing is to train your ability to detach. Learn to do this with every sense, thought, and emotion; with every generated reality; and with whatever your mind presents to you as real. This will not only help you assert control at will, but it will also enable you to enter the deepest realms of your mind without fear of being impacted by it.

Learning to meditate is like training for a marathon: you have to be dedicated to your training and train your body so you make it to the finish line. You must first train yourself to detach, meaning you must first be able to distinguish yourself from any experience in life and to recognise self as consciousness, not just body and mind, before you are ready to take on the challenge of transcendence. Learn to assert control and detach from illusion until you uncover the path towards the truth.

CHAPTER 3

QUICK START GUIDED MEDITATION

Now that you have a general overview of what meditation is, it is time to try it out for yourself. This guided meditation is beginner-friendly and the downloadable audio (link below) is set to fifteen minutes. If using the audio, I recommend that you listen to the guided instruction through noise-cancelling headphones for a better experience.

Note: Read through and get familiar with the instructions first.

To download audio of this guided meditation, visit meditatethebook.com/starterpack

— START OF MEDITATION —

1. Get into a comfortable seated position and ensure your spine is self-supported.

2. Concentrate on an object that is directly in front of you and hold your gaze onto it.

3. Start breathing consciously through your nose. Focus all your attention on your breath, ensuring each inhale is equal to each exhale and that you are breathing comfortably.

4. When your attention is on your breath, close your eyes.

5. On the next inhale, intuitively roll your eyes up towards the centre of your mind without strain. This is a subtle movement and barely noticeable; if you experience any strain, relax your eyes and release the tension.

6. Continue breathing consciously and maintain your focus on your breath.

7. If you get distracted by a sense, thought, or an emotion, simply return awareness back to the breath, and again, on the next inhale, intuitively roll your eyes up towards the centre of your mind.

8. Continue practising for [desired number of minutes] or until you feel at ease and in control.

9. Before you awaken, rub your hands together and then place your palms over your eyes.

10. When ready to awaken, draw your hands down your face and mindfully let the light filter in through your fingers.

— END OF MEDITATION —

This guided meditation is a quick way to reduce stress and harness control of consciousness and is not representative of a substantial meditation practice. To meditate effectively and access the nether regions of the mind and the higher realms of awareness, it is recommended that you prepare mindfully and treat each meditation as a crucial component of life as you do sleep.

CHAPTER 4

PREPARING TO MEDITATE

In meditation, it is as if you are raising consciousness like a hot-air balloon. The balloon represents consciousness, and your breath represents the fire which generates the hot air to raise it. Without breath, consciousness will shrink like the balloon without air, but with it, consciousness, like the balloon, rises. First, ensure that you can breathe fully and consciously. Clear any nasal congestion and avoid meditating in dusty, damp, and cold rooms.

Additionally, just like a hot-air balloon needs to detach from the ropes that hold it down, consciousness needs to detach from the experiences which keep it, you, held down. Preparing to meditate is like loosening the ropes so you can raise consciousness into higher realms of awareness much more conveniently.

As soon as you are inside the hot-air balloon, in a position to meditate, you will want to be as close to taking off as you can. You will want to spend more time raising consciousness and less time settling it, by having to detach from needless sensations, thoughts, and emotions. For example, if you are new to meditation and your body cannot sit in a position for too long, then it would be a shame to waste the time allocated to your meditation trying to get comfortable. This time would be better spent doing yoga and preparing to meditate.

PREPARE YOUR BODY

Always ensure that your body is in good health and do not attempt to sit through physical pain unnecessarily. If physical pain is present, attend to it and ensure that you do not cause yourself any additional harm. Yoga is an excellent way to prepare the body for meditation and in Chapter 7, Step 2 Position, you will learn more about the ideal position of your body for meditation.

Everything in your life that you can sense as real can be considered an attachment. Closing your eyes is the first thing that you can do to immediately shut out a significant amount of physical reality and detach from outer light. Your other senses pose the same problem: they attach you to physical reality.

PREPARE THE ENVIRONMENT

Meditating in a silent room that is dimly lit and fragrance-free may also make meditation easier. Although if you are not used to sitting silently with your mind, directing your senses inwardly can be an overwhelming experience and can encourage you to latch onto physical distractions. Play around with your meditation setting and create an ideal space that works with you. Let your senses take charge and create a setting that helps them to settle.

Light background music and white noise can help settle the mind and ground the sense to hear. Classical flute music and the sound of Tibetan singing bowls are effective too. However, if you are brand new to meditation and are finding it difficult to detach from sound, feel free to add an acoustic accompaniment that resonates with the mood you are trying to attain. Your favourite song or playlist perhaps.

Incense and air infusers can be a way to ground the sense of smell and can also help to keep any flying insects at bay too. Sandalwood is a scent commonly used in temples around the world and the lavender scent is widely known to promote a relaxed state of mind.

Adjust the temperature of your space to an optimal level. In deeper states of meditation, the senses can become more sensitive and the smallest draft can feel like a strong chill, so you may want to wrap yourself in a blanket or keep one nearby. Wrapping yourself snug in a blanket can also help you feel calm and comforted too.

Treat meditation as a therapeutic process and you will soon learn how to relax into your meditation. Your meditation space should be a place where you feel completely safe and secure so you can freely be vulnerable and focus all of your attention within. Meditating out in nature and grounding your senses to the natural environment is an excellent way to meditate, and one I highly recommend.

PREPARE YOUR MIND

You may also want to start reducing the number of nonessential things that consciousness can attach itself to. For example, if you cannot take your mind off of doing the dishes, then do the dishes. Resolve the conflict and then return to your meditation. Common sense will certainly make meditation a much easier practice, so complete your chores, pay your bills, fulfil your basic needs, and clear your mind of clutter prior to meditating. In addition to preparing to meditate, I have found taking action to resolve unnecessary chatter is also a great productivity tool.

To meditate is to take a conscious moment out of your experience of life. The world will not stop creating because you have entered a meditation; the Earth will continue to orbit the sun and time will continue to pass. You are not trying to silence or shut out the world; you are trying to venture into realms beyond it. Let the world be.

WHEN AND WHERE TO MEDITATE

Since detaching from your senses only means to stop giving them attention, a familiar space can make it easier to focus attention away from the outer world. Furthermore, you do not want to be dealing with disruptions and the demands of your everyday life while meditating. Thus, it may be useful to schedule a regular time to meditate in a dedicated meditation space and start forming a routine.

Time of day will not matter at the beginning stages of your practice, though meditating during sunrise will certainly help you prepare for your day. Meditating during the midday sun can help you rejuvenate and refresh your mind, and meditating during the setting sun can help you reset and reflect.

SECTION 2

BEGINNING TO MEDITATE

CHAPTER 5

THE FIVE-STEP PROCESS

The five-step process is about training your mind and body to meditate.

Step 1 Breathe: learning about and engaging your control breath, a state of breathing which helps you identify and set your control state of mind.

Step 2 Position: learning how to sit in meditation and developing your ideal meditation posture.

Step 3 Lock: learning how to turn awareness away from your life and into your meditation.

Step 4 Meditate: understanding how to sustain your meditation and exercise detachment.

Step 5 Integrate: integrating the experience and awakening from your meditative state.

DEVELOPING THE PROCESS

I developed the five-step process during a troubling period in my life. I could not effectively meditate because I was finding it difficult to detach from material conflicts. I had just ended a relationship, had looming money issues after a recent purchase of a house, and was battling anxiety. I was also out of practice; I had not meditated effectively for over ten years.

I was sitting out on my deck looking up at the full moon, wondering why life was not getting any easier. As a kid, whenever I felt lost or alone, I would investigate the sky at night. I would count the stars and document the phases of the moon. I did not have many friends growing up so the big white pie in the sky always felt like a familiar acquaintance. I would meditate, always trying to reach the moon.

I used to look forward to nightfall because everyone was fast asleep, so the world just felt so much bigger and much kinder to be in. I used to think that the Earth was a giant eyeball and that daytime meant that eye was open and the world was awake. Whereas at night, it meant that the eye was closed and that the giant eye had turned around and locked into its meditation, turning awareness away from life and towards the cosmos.

During that moment on the deck, I was regressing to my childhood ways of coping because I was feeling alone. After university, I had learned to use sex, drugs, and spending money as a replacement for meditation to cope with life's challenges. However, just like everything else in the material world, their effectiveness came with an expiration date too.

I was also remembering some of the most awe-inspiring meditation moments of my life. I remembered connecting with deities and how they used to take me to other worlds to sing and dance. I remembered feeling like I could travel back in time, into a past life when I was sitting around a guru telling tales of gods and flying chariots. I remembered how I was never bored when I meditated and how the experience of life always seemed far more straightforward in comparison.

Although I had passed off those experiences as a child as having a wild imagination, meditating never failed to separate me from my troubles. So, I thought I would give meditation a go again, if at least to clear my mind. I figured it would be like riding a bike: I would stumble a little bit and then I would be able to soar beyond the cosmos with ease and control.

However, every time I attempted to lock into a meditation, I was gripped by my stress-inducing thoughts—thoughts like wanting to escape my life and how much I felt trapped because of the weight of my growing debt. I was also thinking randomly about the lights I may have left on inside the house, what snacks I could make from the ingredients in my fridge, and when best to fill my car up with gas.

I used to experience awe within mere moments of sitting in meditation, yet here I was struggling to let go of the most arbitrary of thoughts. So, stubbornly I tried again: I shook off the tension, reset my focus to breathing, realigned my spine, rolled my eyes back up, and attempted to lock into a meditation.

When I focused on another thought, or an annoying sound or other sensation, I caught myself getting frustrated. So, then I stubbornly started again. I focused on my breath—placing it ahead of the sense, thought, or emotion—repositioned my body, and locked back into meditation.

I kept returning to the meditation. Breathe, position, lock, and meditate. I repeated this instruction for about forty-five minutes, each time with more determination than the last until it became a commanding instruction from my mind to my body: Breathe. Position. Lock. Meditate.

Then something wild happened. I felt as if I was sitting on the moon and looking back at myself sitting on my deck meditating. I could still hear the thoughts telling my body to 'Breathe. Position. Lock. Meditate', but I was not creating them; it was as if I left them there like an echo from the ring of a pooja bell. This state I was in felt familiar, but as soon as I started to think about why it was familiar instead of trusting and being in the experience of it, I went right back inside my body thinking about memories from my childhood.

I do not know what it was about that experience particularly, but I felt something within myself shift. It had felt like I had broken a seal or cleared a roadblock. It felt more expansive than it felt out of the body. Whatever it was, it felt right, it felt natural and true. Though it did not last long at all, barely even a few seconds, it was enough to silence my mind. I felt incredibly still and content.

Before opening my eyes and awakening from my meditation, I wanted to ensure that I had soaked in this experience and savoured it. I relived the experience in my mind like a memory. I wanted to store the knowledge of how I got there and what it took to get there and save the awareness as a measurement against my next meditation. I wanted every fibre of my physical being to feel what I had felt, and it made me think carefully about what I should do when I open my eyes, and the fifth step, integration, was born.

YOUR MEDITATION JOURNEY

At the beginning stages of your meditation practice, consider the five-step process as nothing more than a suggested training manual, like a series of stretches that make up a yoga set. As you progress and begin to successfully detach, you may find yourself adjusting the process, adding or removing steps, or developing an entirely new process for yourself. Understand that you are free to do so.

You can also use what you are about to learn as a framework to develop your own meditation techniques and write your own guided meditations. Please note that you should always progress at your own pace, and do not force yourself beyond your own capabilities. Just like yoga, listen to your body first and follow the instruction of the teacher second.

I cannot guarantee that you will end up on the moon as I did. As far as I understand, my landing on the moon was just content that my consciousness had access to, to construct a context for the experience I was having. Furthermore, do keep practising. Do not expect transcendental results immediately, for effective meditation requires training and trust.

The five-step process is designed to help you detach and take command of your mind so you can begin to deconstruct reality, release consciousness from the prison that is the mind, and enter into a broader realm of inner experience.

CHAPTER 6

STEP I BREATHE

The first step in meditation is to engage your control breath. Your control breath is simply a conscious inhale and exhale through your nose, in equal measure, at a comfortable and controlled rate. If you find it difficult to breathe through your nose, try to clear any nasal congestion. Breathing through your nose enables you to elongate your breath with much more control, allowing you to keep consciousness (awareness) alive, as it enters heightened and unknown realms of existence beyond any experience of life.

In the Vedic scriptures, there is a term often associated with breath called prana. Prana means life energy or vital principle, and though it is often mistaken as breath, prana is technically the energy that your breath carries. According to ancient Sanskrit literature, all things in creation carry prana in order to exist and be in physical life. Think of prana like magic that gives life and think of breathing like a pump that keeps the magic alive. Control breathing simply means to be consciously in control of the pump, taking back command from whatever else took charge of it, like a distraction or your state of mind.

Breathing carries an incredible responsibility because it carries prana. The fact that you can breathe means that you have a vital and active role in keeping all life in motion, and in constant creation. Notice how not one living being can sustain their own prana. You need the Earth just as much as the Earth needs you, and this design ensures balance and the preservation of life.

Every inhale preserves you and every exhale preserves the earth, and this is the divine responsibility we all share. It is an equal partnership that we have with all living things. Each life is said to sustain another life however large or small the being. All life is said to be of equal value, for you are just as equally as alive as a bee or a plant for instance. The only thing that differs is the ability of the body that life exists in. Respectively, the body determines the force of breath, the force of breath determines the force of life, and consciousness can control this force enabling you to create.

When meditating, it is important to feel as if you exist in life as breath, as a force that gives life to creation. As your vital organs operate and exist to serve your body, your whole body operates and exists simply to serve your breath, which serves the will of consciousness. Consider your breath as the physical form of consciousness instead of your body.

Your body is like the magic wand that sustains breath, which sustains the flow of prana, the magic that consciousness uses to create and give life. You are more valuable as breath than you are as a body, in fact, your body without breath is incredibly useless, like a magic wand without magic. Learn to exist as breath in life, and your body and your mind will soon learn to obey.

USING BREATH TO DETACH

Focusing on your breathing makes detaching from your senses, your thoughts, and your emotions much easier because each of these experiences is a mere creation sustained by breath. Existing as breath enables you to realise your power as a force of preservation, a force that can give life to a creation and keep it alive.

Breath is more important to life than anything else in physical or metaphysical existence. As long as you are breathing, you are incredibly valuable to the preservation of life and if you are breathing consciously, you are more consciously involved in the preservation of life. Alternatively, restricting breath can act like a force of destruction, restricting something from manifesting in life.

TIP!

Do yourself a favour the next time you feel sad, anxious, scared, or develop any other negative emotion which causes discomfort. Close your eyes, hold your breath for thirty – ninety seconds to assert control, and then engage conscious breathing. The likes of anxiety, fear, paranoia, and panic are no match to the power of breath. Panic attacks and anxiety attacks are the results of a thought that has gotten control of or ahead of your breath. As I tell my clients, you can choose to either breathe consciously or let your mental disorder control your life, the choice is truly yours.

Learn to prioritise and place your breath ahead of every sense, thought, and emotion, and you will command control of your life and your state of being. When meditating, the only thing you need to accept as real is your breath and any truth which serves the preservation of life. If there is something in your mind that restricts you from living your life peacefully, destructive thoughts for example, replace it with breath and repeat until you have control and have harnessed the power of creation. Replacing mental illness with mental health starts with the breath. Lead with breath and your life will follow.

USING BREATH TO CREATE

Though it may be difficult to believe, breathing is much more than just inhaling oxygen and exhaling carbon dioxide. From a meditative standpoint, your breath also carries with it a lot of data. Data that is exchanged between your outer world, life, and your inner world, reality. If your inner world is anxious, your experience of the outer world will be too and vice versa.

Think about the energy that resides in your mind when you are happy in comparison to the energy that resides in your mind when you are sad. Realise how differently you experience and interpret the world based on either state of mind. If you are happy, the world is a happy place to be; whereas if you are sad, the world is a sad place to be. Your emotional state dictates the experience regardless of the event unfolding. It's like a feedback loop, and occurrences in your life can also have an impact on your emotional state too.

On the other hand, notice how the collective energy of the world can have an impact on your state of mind. For instance, you can get angry at what you see on the news, you can feel insecure because of something you see on social media, and an advertisement can influence your decision and your state of mind. Focusing on the breath is to focus on this feedback loop, this exchange of data, like a cyclical connection to all life on Earth, a connection that determines all life's collective evolutionary direction. You aren't the only one creating magic and casting spells.

Think of it like this, when you inhale, you inhale the energy of the collective state of the world, which influences and gives life to whatever is on your mind. When you exhale, the state of your mind is energy inhaled by nature, like the plants and the trees, impacting their inner state, which is then exhaled and inhaled by other life-forms and so the cycle continues. It's like a form of communication which directs and determines the energy of life on the planet. When breathing consciously, you have more control of how life turns out; if you are not breathing consciously, the state of life determines how you turn out.

Life is in a constant state of creation kept in motion with every inhale and exhale. Though incredibly subtle, each breath potentially carries creational data and being aware of this exchange can help you consciously maintain a constructive mindset. Your life can be what you want it to be and it starts with being present with your breath.

You must oversee your state in life, instead of allowing the state of life to determine your state of being. This is one of the first critical developments gained by meditating: the ability to create and experience the life of your choosing. You may also choose to consider the life that you have been presented with as the challenge you need to overcome for your conscious entity to evolve.

YOUR CONTROL BREATH

Pay attention to what rate and pace of breath enable you to sustain a healthy and comfortable mindset, and this should be set as your control breath. Let it be a comfortable inhale and exhale, at equal measure, and at your lungs' full capacity. Whenever you engage your control breath, you are consciously restoring your control state of being. When faced with a racing mind, for instance, control breathing is how you can settle it.

Furthermore, knowing your control state allows you to measure every inner and outer experience of life against it. If ever life starts to feel out of your control, you can simply breathe and start reigning it in. Knowing your control breath and restoring your control state can keep you sane and safe as you venture beyond your zones of comfort. This is a skill you will need if you are going to transcend beyond reality and question your truths in meditation.

Practise your control breath frequently. For example, when you are shopping at the grocery store, exercise a control breath before placing each item in your basket. When in traffic, keep engaging your control breath to keep your frustrations at bay and maintain your control state. When in meditation, always engage your control breath when faced with a creation of the mind which does not serve or enlighten you.

Imagine living your life only paying attention to your breath. Your control breath can be the literal force on which you build your life around, the force of your life's creation. The moment you realise that you are not in conscious control of your breath, you can start to raise awareness on what it was that took your breath away and assess the validity of the reality you are experiencing. This is an excellent practice for those with trust and commitment issues.

No matter the experience of life, positive or negative, good or bad, inner or outer, knowing what gains control of your breath can teach you how the controlling force impacts your life. In such a moment, you check in with yourself and examine if the experience is healthy or not. Remember, where life is concerned, preservation is key; breath is the vital preserver, and if something else has taken hold of it, it should at least be something of equal value to the preservation of life; anything less is destructive and anything more is creative. Measure against the preservation of life and integrate with reality wisely.

Control breathing puts you in control of your experience of life so you never need to be afraid to evolve and explore beyond what you know. If ever in doubt, put consciousness back in control of breath and let go of everything else.

Breathe, recover, restore clarity and peace of mind, and then proceed.

 Step 1. Engage your control breath

CHAPTER 7
STEP 2 POSITION

A SELF-SUPPORTED SPINE

Once you have established your control breath, listen to the sensations in your body and establish a comfortable meditation position. The major component of a meditation position is an upright and self-supported spine. If the spine is not self-supported, then your body may enter a state of rest and you may end up falling asleep, and trying to remain conscious with a rested spine takes effort and energy away from processing thought and practising detachment. Let your body keep you awake so consciousness can deal with your mind. More importantly, the significance of a self-supported spine is to ensure that you are conscious during the meditative state so you can attain the knowledge gained from your conscious travels and remember the experience.

Furthermore, a straight and self-supported spine puts you in a robust position that cannot be easily influenced or swayed by the illusions of the mind. Like a tree that can withstand strong winds, a strong meditation position means you are ready to handle whatever your mind presents. As my mum would say, 'A strong position is a proud position'; show your mind that you are proud of present life and that there is nothing it can create to make you fall.

You will often notice that when you wake up from sleep, you do not remember much of what went on inside your mind during it. That is the key difference between meditation and sleep: meditation is a conscious process, whereas sleep is an unconscious one. Holding your spine upright keeps you awake so you can venture into the depths of your mind without losing consciousness. Therefore, the first step in establishing your meditation position is assessing how best to position yourself.

You can effectively meditate standing up, sitting on a chair or cushion, or ideally, on the floor with your legs crossed. The significance of sitting on the floor is to ground yourself as if you are electrically charging your body. The most ideal meditation position is called the lotus position, which involves sitting on the floor, crossed-legged, with each foot resting on the top of the opposite thigh. This position is ideal because it reduces the amount of strain on your legs and feet, and it keeps the spine upright and your body self-supported.

The lotus position can be helpful with deep states of meditation and advanced meditation practices because you will likely be sitting in meditation for lengthy periods of time. Do not worry if you cannot sit into the lotus position, just ensure that you are comfortable holding your spine upright. Keep in mind that any pain or tension within the body will significantly retract consciousness from your meditation as your body will demand your attention, like a bungee cord yanking you back from falling, or in this case rising. Therefore, develop your position to limit any stress on your body.

Yoga and Pilates improve flexibility and spinal posture and are excellent ways to train the body into a comfortable meditation position. As you develop your practice, you will feel encouraged to improve your posture and will realise the benefits of the lotus position. For now, any position that is comfortable and allows you to support your own spine will suffice. If you do struggle to support your spine, however, you may use a cushion to support your lower back so it sits upright.

If you can sit on the floor cross-legged, you can add additional support to your back and knees with cushions. If you rest the base of your spine on the front of a firm pillow, bolster, or meditation cushion and have your hips raised above your knees, you will find it much more comfortable sitting on the floor. Also, you may want to add cushioned support under your knees and lighten the weight on your feet to prevent them from falling asleep.

If you think of what it would feel like to sit upright and cross-legged on a cloud, it may help you better position the pillows more comfortably. Be sure to listen to your body and adjust your posture; accordingly, be comfortable and ensure your spine is self-supported. If you simply cannot support your spine because of injury or disability, you can also lie down. However, in this situation, keep your eyes open and focus on the ceiling so you don't fall asleep and deepen your control breath and breathe with your stomach to maintain conscious energy flow.

EYES CLOSED

Once into position, close your eyes and rest your hands wherever comfortable. Closing your eyes prepares you to turn awareness inward. It is the quickest way to shut out the light and focus your attention on the goings-on in your mind. When the sun goes down, the skies open to reveal the cosmos and enable you to see further into the universe. This is the significance of closing your eyes: you are seeking the light within the darkness.

The transcendent state is to connect with the light within; therefore, if the light outside of the body is commanding more attention, then consciousness will struggle to travel deeper within. Exploring your whole inner world is like looking into the cosmos and studying each star, and to do so successfully, especially for the very distant truths, you will want to limit light. The other reason for closing your eyes is so you can safely follow through with the next step, locking, where you will learn how to roll your eyes up and turn awareness in.

HAND POSITION

If you are a beginner, you can place your hands anywhere they feel comfortably rested. You can place them on your thighs, clasp them in front of you, or you can rest one hand on top of the other.

If you are an intermediate meditator, then I would recommend placing one hand on top of the other to help balance out your mind's operation. Think of this hand position as counteracting the way your mind processes information to balance out its operation; for example, if you are a freethinker, switching your hands' instinctual position can influence more critical thought, aiding new and alternative perspectives. It feels different; therefore, it can encourage you to think differently.

EXERCISE

To know which way is best for you, instinctually place one hand on top of the other and then switch them around. Whatever you did instinctually can be representative of your mind's default way of operating; therefore, switching the hands will help balance and centre the mind.

If you are an advanced meditator, you may want to adopt a mudra. A mudra is a nerve-stimulating hand position, the most popular of which being the gyan mudra. The gyan mudra places each hand on each knee, with your arms stretched outright, and your index finger and your thumb pressing into each other. The remaining three fingers are consciously stretched out. This mudra is designed specifically for accessing wisdom and the storing of knowledge.

There are many different types of mudras and each one of them carries a specific benefit. Mudras can support health, promote prosperity, or support a specific emotional state. Each finger is associated with a natural element and the various combinations guide energy in a specific way. Starting from the thumb and moving across, the elements are fire, air, ether, earth, and water.

TIP!

If you liken each element to the strings on a violin, each mudra position is like pressing down on a string to select a pitch. Each pitch provides a different frequency which stimulates the energy within the body in different ways. Do not worry too much about mudras until you advance your practice.

SPINAL POSTURE

Another thing to note is your spinal posture. Think of your spine like the bow of a bow and arrow and imagine the string on the bow linking the top of your head down to your anus. The string represents a flow of energy.

The ideal spinal posture is when the energy, the string, is vertically straight so the energy flows easily. If your back curves too far forward, the flow of energy will be strained, and if your back curves too far backwards, the energy gathers. To measure the alignment of your posture, hold up your chest comfortably, and align the top of your head with your anus for good energy flow.

If you think of the centre of your chest as the centre of the bow from which you shoot the arrow, then you may be able to find and set your ideal spinal posture. You can adjust your seat, your spine, your chest, and the level of your chin to help with the alignment of your spine. Aim to level your chin to a 180-degree angle and ensure your overall posture is even, shoulder to shoulder, head to anus, as if to form a cross. A weak posture may result in what I call a limp meditation: if the flow of energy is weak, consciousness will struggle to rise.

If you are dedicated to your meditation practice, you will find yourself directing your yogic exercises to strengthen your meditation position. When accessing heightened states of awareness, maximise your experience and do not let the meditation be cut short because of a stress signal from the body. Also, learn to meditate without the support of anything but the earth your body sits upon so you can comfortably lock into your meditation in any place and at any time.

 Step 1. Engage your control breath

 Step 2. Enter your meditation position

CHAPTER 8
STEP 3 LOCK

To lock into your meditation, close your eyes and as you inhale, roll your eyes up without strain or any tension to wherever they settle comfortably. This is a subtle and gentle movement. Forcing your eyes too far beyond their natural position can cause permanent damage, so <u>do not strain your eyes beyond where they settle comfortably and engage at your own risk.</u>

Rolling your eyes up indicates that you are shifting awareness away from creation and towards the creator, from the physical experience of life to the metaphysical experience of life and beyond. Think of this motion as navigating conscious awareness into your inner world and away from the outer one that is experienced with your body.

You mustn't force your eyes to stay locked into your meditation; by doing so, you are technically returning to the experience of your body and rendering your meditation ineffective. If you find yourself venturing into uncontrolled thought, distracted by a physical sensation, or perhaps overcome by an emotion, you have disengaged your meditative state. If this is the case, you will need to reassert conscious control with breath and lock back into your meditation.

As you regularly enter meditative states and strengthen your practice, you may notice that your eyes will naturally be drawn further back into your head without any conscious aid or effort. If you have ever witnessed someone in a trance-like state, you may have noticed that their eyes roll back almost effortlessly. Locking is like giving this trance-like state a little nudge to engage your meditation (to reiterate, this is a subtle and gentle movement which must not cause any strain or tension, if it does you are trying too hard).

THE THIRD-EYE FOCUS

Think of locking into your meditation as a symbolic gesture, whereby your regular eyes hand over conscious control to your third eye, the term *third eye* is a metaphorical term used to comprehend the awareness of insight. The third eye is the sixth chakra and probably the closest thing you have to a sixth sense.

Think of your regular eyes as *outsight* for comparison, and your third eye as the sense that governs all your senses and experiences in life. Whenever you have personal thoughts, like thinking about a problem in your life or what you would say to someone you like, consider this your third eye in action.

Locking is what I would also refer to as the *third-eye focus*. Consider the third eye as the sense of self or the sense of truth. Arguably, it is the eye of the creator or the *creator's eye*, which enables you to reimagine worlds outside of your physical experience of life.

The third eye is like the eye you would use in your dreams, imagination, memories, and ideas. It grants you the ability to develop your reality and outlook on life. The third eye can also be referred to as the eye of truth, and when fully engaged and open, it grants you the ability to see beyond illusion and creation, which is why you meditate from the third eye's perspective.

Your ability to sense truth improves with each meditation because your third eye opens a little more each time that you successfully meditate, so do keep practising. The third eye opens fully when transcendence is experienced because once you have experienced the ultimate truth, *the supreme creator*, or whatever or whoever you realise it to be, you can't unknow it. Living life with the third eye fully open is the enlightened state of being.

In ancient literature and psychedelic art, the third eye is often depicted in the middle of the forehead, but these depictions are the only representative of an enlightened state of being. If the term *third eye* were more of a literal concept, I would guess that it is referencing the pineal gland, though what it exactly is or is referring to I cannot be certain.

I would like to reiterate one last time, that locking into your meditation should not cause you any physical strain or tension. Do not push your eyes beyond their physical capabilities. By doing so, you may risk causing permanent damage to your eyes, and any tension or strain will only hinder your ability to meditate.

- ✓ Step 1. Engage your control breath
- ✓ Step 2. Enter your meditation position
- ✓ **Step 3. Lock into your meditation**

CHAPTER 9
STEP 4 MEDITATE

The first time that you lock, in an attempt to meditate, you may only find yourself in a state of meditation for a mere fraction of a millisecond before involuntarily getting reattached to something presented by your mind or body. Meditation takes practise and the moment you find yourself attached, repeat steps 1–4 and begin again.

Briefly speaking, to know when you are effectively meditating is to recognise that you, consciousness, are a distinctly separate entity from any experience of life. This includes anything in your present waking state, any experience relived in memory, and any perceived experience directing your life.

At the early stages of your meditation practice, you are aiming to observe all and any experience that your mind presents to you as a creation. Then, once objectivity is achieved, you can begin assessing the creation, realising the source of it, and successfully detaching from it. This is when you can restore your mental health and recover mindful function because you are no longer gripped by the reality of what your mind has created.

As you advance your practice, you will be able to raise awareness to study larger constructs of reality, such as life and death, as creations too. As you can effectively detach and recognise the elusive nature of reality, you will find yourself sitting in a state of stillness, like being inside an empty glass elevator momentarily shut off from the world.

It is in this state that you begin, or attempt to begin, your transcendental journey. For you will have successfully carried consciousness away from the experience of the body, of the mind, and towards what is known as the soul. Once consciousness resides in the soul, you are ready to ascend into higher realms of awareness that cannot be accessed with a body or realised within the constraints of the mind.

The mind is like a conscious control centre that generates a reality instructing you on what to do based on the data it receives from your senses and memories. If reattachment occurs quickly and you find yourself distracted or consumed by the reality in your mind, it is likely because the nature of yourself as body is truer to you than the nature of yourself as consciousness. In other words, the finite nature of life and death of the body is far more real to you than the infinite nature of consciousness and creation.

Struggling to meditate is a failure to recognise yourself as an entity far greater than your mind and body. If your trust in whatever you are experiencing in your mind is far greater than you, the conscious entity that is experiencing it, then you will get pulled out of your meditative state and into the reality conceived by your mind. Remember, inside your mind, your body does not exist; you are not carrying anything from physical life into your mind. In your mind, you can only exist as consciousness.

TRAINING CONSCIOUSNESS

Imagine that locking into your meditation is like finding yourself inside a very busy office floor of a company that you own. The windows and doors to the outside world represent the world around your body, and inside the office represents your mind. Your goal as the owner of this company is to get from one end of the office and into the elevator on the other end, without getting distracted or pulled away by anything demanding your attention. Once inside the elevator, where you can go is an infinite number of possibilities, for you, consciousness, have isolated yourself from the demands of your body and the distractions of your mind.

When you find yourself getting distracted and attached to a sense, thought, or an emotion, it's like you've been pulled out of the elevator, and repeating steps 1 – 4—breathe, position, lock, meditate—is like resetting your journey back towards the elevator, attempting to get back into that state of stillness. Each time you repeat the steps, you will get wiser to the distractions, enabling you to recognise and detach from them much more quickly and enter states of stillness for longer and longer periods at a time.

At the beginning stages of your meditation practice, you may feel like you have to respond to each call for your attention; however, as you improve your practice, you will learn to only respond to, or choose to only respond to, specific requests from the mind and body that you deem important, if wanting to respond at all.

TIP!

As a precaution, please ensure that you do respond to any physical pain or tension so as to not cause any harm to your body. In step 2 position, when you repeat this step, it is an opportunity for you to readjust your body into a more comfortable meditation position. In time you will realise your most ideal position that will enable you to lock into longer meditations, allowing you to skip this step altogether.

Meditation sitting does not have to mean one attempt to meditate, and much like sleep, meditation can occur in cycles too. So, don't stress if you get distracted or consumed by something, when you realise you've become attached, just repeat the cycle: breathe, position, lock, and meditate, and over time you will find yourself needing to repeat these steps less frequently as you learn how *you* meditate.

Even in deep states of meditation, something in your mind or body may command your attention and will momentarily pull you back from your meditative state; this is normal. However, because you have trained and improved your practice, you can take a moment to assess the reality and decide if it indeed requires your immediate attention or not. If not (most likely not), you can simply detach and lock back into your meditation with ease and pick up where you left off with conscious precision like a meditation master!

You have probably already experienced this ascent and descent of consciousness. For instance, if someone has tried waking you up from a deep state of sleep, notice how their voice gets louder and more prominent as consciousness descends from your sleeping state and back to your waking state. Raising consciousness in meditation is much like this except you are aware and in control, you can consciously choose not to descend from your meditative state and reject the echoes coming from your mind and body.

THE STATE OF REALITY

Reality is simply whatever moment consciousness is existing in. That moment can be in your waking life when consciousness is existing near your physical senses. It can be in a memory or deep thought when consciousness is existing nearer or in your subconscious mind, and it can also be in a dream state or perceived reality if consciousness is residing idly inside your mind. Whatever consciousness is experiencing and is attached too, that's reality.

Meditation is to consciously move out of that moment to observe it. Based on the observation you can choose to accept it and integrate it into your life; or, you can reject it and continue to raise consciousness beyond it. To observe, again, just breathe consciously and with control and repeat as necessary, especially for stubborn realities that induce anxiety and fear.

Even a simple noise can generate a whole new reality in your mind, and to improve your meditation and recognise your reality as a creation, try and capture and witness the process of its construction. If one variable of this construction were to change, then you would be able to recognise the elusive nature of the reality, detach, and move on from it without having to repeat the steps.

For example, if you are meditating and you hear someone walk through a door, that sound can generate a whole reality within your mind. From the construction around the sound, the door, the development of broader aspects of the door, the room, and the enactment of potential scenarios from who walked through the door to why they did, and so on.

Normally, this construction happens so quickly that you fail to recognise that it is indeed a creation of the mind and easy to accept as real, and before you know it, you're reattached. Regularly practising meditation and exercising detachment can slow this process down. Even just trying to witness the creation of reality in action will significantly improve your ability to meditate and drastically improve your mental health because you are consciously learning how your mind operates and responds to the world.

When dealing with a reality in your mind that is having an emotional grip, for example, reliving a childhood trauma, then regain control with breath. Once back in conscious control, you can choose to integrate the control state and awaken, or lock back into your meditation, consciously reviving the memory. You can then start to play with the details of its construction to realise its elusive nature, and potentially loosen the emotional grip.

EXERCISE

Think about a room in your house and now imagine tearing off the ceiling to reveal the sky. Change the colour of the walls and place yourself in the middle of the room as a dinosaur. In meditation, you are a creator witnessing creation, and as the creator, you are also able to create.

What is on your mind is yours to decide; it is a creation that you have full control over, so if a creation is causing you trouble, breathe, lock back into your meditation, and realise that it is not in control, you are. Revive the memory and change the details to recognise its elusive nature and once the illusion is no longer able to grip you, recreate the memory, the illusion, observe it, and learn from it.

To learn, you can simply raise questions to it, such as: How did you get there? Why are you causing so much trouble? How can I let you go? Connect to it as if it has a life of its own separate from you. This can help you to detach from any rigid beliefs or stubborn memories that are negatively impacting your life, granting you more conscious control and a more present experience of life.

For instance, if a person was suffering from PTSD because of abuse, then the person could reshape the energy of the abuser to something far less threatening. A client once revived a memory of childhood abuse and consciously shrunk their abuser down to the size of a grain of rice. At that moment, the client could limit the impact of the memory, realising that it was a memory affecting them and not the present moment. This enabled them to release themselves from the grip of the abuse, regain conscious control, and be more present in life. Remember if all else fails, reset the process and harness control with breath. It will take practise.

Always keep in mind that your body is physically sitting safely in meditation, and whatever your mind is presenting to you as real is merely an illusion. Furthermore, this is not to say you are manipulating or changing your memory, to do so, you would have to carry out this process repeatedly until you believe what you have created to be the memory instead. This changing of variables is to help you harness your conscious independence; it will not help you alter your memories for you are consciously involved in the process. Each alteration essentially creates a memory of the alteration, the mind is impressively a safe space to be in.

Your emotions are an indicator of an attachment. If you are having an emotional response in your meditation, then you have accepted something as real and are allowing it to rule your life. Even if you find yourself getting frustrated at unnecessary and arbitrary thoughts, realise that you are gripped by an illusion. Your body is not there, you are not there, you simply think you are. Remember—breathe, position, lock, and meditate and repeat as necessary, chipping away the attachment with each round.

Anything in your mind can be controlled and limiting conscious experience to life and the confines of the mind are minor in comparison to what you can truly achieve in meditation. Don't be fooled by an illusion and certainly don't live your life by one.

PRACTISE, PRACTISE, PRACTISE!

Whenever you find yourself attached, just repeat the process and breathe, reposition if you need to, and lock back into your meditation. Keep practising these steps repeatedly and learn to prioritise and place breath ahead of every sense, thought, and emotion. Place breath ahead of any generated reality that your mind can construct and assert conscious control. With enough practise, you will find yourself in such control of your mind that you will be able to keep the likes of anxiety, fear, and paranoia at bay.

The moment when you realise that you are gripped by a formed reality, that you are having an experience and not observing one, is the moment you breathe consciously and attempt to lock back into your meditation. This is how you can train yourself to meditate and develop an independent state of consciousness, separate from the operations of your mind and functions of your body.

A state whereby you can witness how and why this reality is being constructed, instead of existing inside the reality itself. To witness the creation instead of existing as part of it helps to raise self-awareness and can even grant you the ability to assess emotional triggers, all by sitting in contemplation and breathing. Best of all, it does not cost you a penny and you can do this anywhere and at any time.

IN SUMMARY

This process is about training your mind to carry consciousness out of reality and into objectivity. When you reengage your control breath, you are essentially retrieving consciousness back from reality and separating yourself from the experience, as if to create a wedge.

Then, you can reposition your body if you need to as sometimes tension in the body can arise. When comfortable again, on the next conscious inhale, roll your eyes back up and lock into your meditation. Simply repeat the process as necessary until you feel some sort of conscious shift.

A conscious shift can be anything from attaining a desired emotional state and clarity of the mind to the realisation of truth and transcendence. With enough practice, you will be able to engage your meditative state at will and distinguish consciousness from conscious experience. It is a lot of information to consume, which is why all you need to concern yourself with is breathing. If you can breathe, you can meditate.

Meditation is like training for a marathon, you don't start out by simply running a marathon. You have to train, build up your stamina, and continuously build on your progress. In the beginning, you are clearing your mind and developing conscious control over your experience of life. Once this ability is attained, you can then begin to detach far more easily and raise consciousness beyond the experiences of the mind, beyond dream-like states, until eventually, you enter transcendence.

In each meditation sitting, keep repeating steps 1 – 4 until you gain some sort of measurable development. Practise enough so you can catch yourself in an attachment quicker and are able to detach and lock into your meditative state, observing in stillness, for longer intervals. Even if you just practise conscious breathing for one minute a day, you will noticeably improve your experience of life and ability to meditate.

All forms of reality and experiences of life technically exist after breath. This is because you can only experience reality when you are breathing. When you return to the breath, you are returning to the very foundation of life, you are returning to a state prior to the construction of reality and before any experience of it. Hence, prioritising and placing breath ahead of any sense, thought, or emotion.

Detachment is a powerful ability to exercise and with it you will start to see mental disorders as mere forms of creation too. With this greater insight, you will be able to reign over your mental health and maybe even eliminate any mental problems altogether.

Breathe, position, lock, and meditate. Repeat as necessary until you have reached a desired state of mind and then start preparing to integrate and awaken from your meditation.

 Step 1. Engage your control breath

 Step 2. Enter your meditation position

 Step 3. Lock into your meditation

 Step 4. Meditate . . .

CHAPTER 10
STEP 5 INTEGRATE

Integration is the final step before awakening from your meditation. It is about giving yourself a moment to restore conscious awareness back to your body and store the awareness you have raised in meditation. It is simply a matter of preparing to awaken from your meditation, as if to consciously wake up from a deep sleep.

To integrate, keep your eyes closed and deepen your control breath to wake up and invigorate the cells inside your body. Then get into a relaxed position. You can rest against a wall or lie down, stretch your legs out, or sit with your knees up. There is no specific way you must be for integration. Integration is simply a personal ritual designed to disengage you from your meditation, wake up your body, and reconnect you to your life, so do feel free to make it your own.

Do be aware of any parts of your body that may have fallen asleep, especially if you have been sitting on your legs and have carried a weight on your feet for some time. It is also important that you do not open your eyes right away, because just like waking up from your sleep, your eyes may need to adjust to the light. To support your eyes, place your palms over your eyes to effectively block out the light. Then open your eyes in this state and slowly slide your hands down your face and allow rays of light to filter in through your fingers.

Integration should not be overlooked because it is where you reinforce mindfulness. Mindfulness is like a by-product of meditation. Where meditation raises awareness, integration allows it to settle into your mind and body so you can integrate the knowledge into your life. Mindfulness is to act in accordance with your truth, to act upon the knowledge gained from having raised awareness in meditation.

Each time you meditate, you are effectively raising consciousness into higher states of awareness. Therefore, every time you awaken from a meditative state, you are waking up wiser than you were before you entered it. Even at the beginning stages of your practice, noticing any little aches and pains in your body and realising the things that were negatively affecting you are micro-levels of truths that you have become aware of and can act upon.

For example, you can exercise your control breath whenever you find yourself stressed and triggered by things occurring in life. You can also direct your physical exercises and yoga practices to treat the root cause of your tension instead of the symptom of it, to strengthen your meditation position, and to eliminate those 'created' aches and pains. Meditation encourages you to observe everything as a creation, and when you also begin assessing negative health issues as such, you can begin piecing together solutions to remedy many of the body's problems.

TIP!

I highly suggest finding a good yoga teacher or personal trainer; however, if you cannot afford the luxury, start researching and learning the sun salutation and begin developing your personal yoga practice. By practising the sun salutation, a five-minute set (approx.) of basic yoga poses, three times a day for at least two weeks, you will significantly improve your posture, flexibility, and stamina and reduce a lot of physical tension that can arise when sitting in meditation.

When you become an intermediate meditator, you will notice your integration ritual evolve into a process of lifting restrictions that may have kept your inner truths at bay. For example, maybe there was something about yourself that you had kept hidden from the world, like your sexuality or a creative expression.

Your integration can be a moment for you to sit with your truth and get comfortable with it as something that is a part of who you truly are. Furthermore, you can utilise your integration ritual to assess what aspects of your life are, or were, contributing to the suppression of your truth. It can give you a moment to truly understand how to act on the truths you have connected with, and how to release them into your life safely and mindfully.

After an advanced practice of meditation, where you are entering more enlightened states of awareness and accessing states of transcendence, the process of integration will likely evolve into a necessity. Your integration ritual will serve as a moment for you to restore inner peace and function, in what can feel like a brand-new world that you are about to awaken into.

Sometimes your integration may need to carry on beyond just a moment to yourself. For instance, you may want to take some time off work or spend a few days on your own to familiarise yourself with this heightened state of being.

Think of your mind and body as operations which serve consciousness. If consciousness is operating at a higher truth frequency than your mind and body were previously used to, then be mindful and allow a moment for your mind and body to catch up and integrate, like a computer rebooting after an update.

Integration is subtle at the beginning, which may encourage you to skip it altogether. However, do try to integrate after every meditation and make it a habit. Developing a solid integration ritual is great preparation for enlightenment, because a successful integration can turn an experience of awe into a moment of acceptance.

In summary, integration is your opportunity to integrate a heightened state of being and prepares you to step into the reality of your creation. It is a personal moment to reassert your role as the creator of your life and to think about what you need to do next in accordance to your truth, which could mean removing a restriction or creating a solution so you can preserve your life and live liberally in truth.

If you have failed to achieve peace of mind, then integration can also be a moment to assess your state of mind and re-enter your meditation if need be—just repeat the steps. It can also serve as a moment to pause from your meditation, if on the rare occasion you feel overwhelmed by the experience. Please do not overlook this final step. Make it a ritual that is yours and allow it to be a moment for you to evaluate and reflect.

Exit your meditation when you feel ready to step back into life.

- ✓ Step 1. Engage your control breath.
- ✓ Step 2. Enter your meditation position.
- ✓ Step 3. Lock into your meditation.
- ✓ Step 4. Meditate . . .
- ✓ **Step 5. Integrate awareness.**

SECTION 3

DEEPENING YOUR MEDITATION

CHAPTER 11

MOVING OUT OF REALITY

To deepen your meditation practice, you will need to consider your life and every construct within your mind as an illusion or a creation that exists independently from you. This includes your body and everything you experience with your physical senses, your memories, your identity, and all your hopes and aspirations too. This is not to say to forget or dismiss any aspect of your life; in meditation your aim is to recognise yourself beyond all and any material elements of life and to recognise yourself, firstly, as consciousness.

When you close your eyes to meditate or sleep, whatever you experience in your mind, understand your body is not physically present there. Your body and all aspects of life remain in physical existence, while you, consciousness, experience a world that is, or worlds that are, separate from physical reality.

For example, if you think about what you had for breakfast this morning, realise that your body is not physically in that memory;

your body is in life reading this book while consciousness is retrieving and recreating the reality of what you had for breakfast. Furthermore, when you are dreaming, realise that your physical body is not present in your dreams either; it is just another reality, an illusion, that exists in addition to your life.

Your physical body literally only exists in the present moment. You cannot move your body into the past or the future, even if you could freeze your body so you could wake up one day in the future, understand that your body would still only be waking up in a present moment, like waking up from sleep after a few hours pass. Consciousness, on the other hand, can move freely throughout time; it can have an experience in the present with your body, relive stored experiences in your past, and can perceive future experiences.

When you enter a memory or have a dream, understand that it is you existing as consciousness and not the body. Anything in your mind is a conscious experience and not a physical one. It can sometimes help to visualise consciousness, yourself, as a ball of energy that sits inside your mind, as the entity that operates your body, visits your past, and constructs your future.

When operating your body, you, as consciousness, are operating in your physical life-form. Consciousness cannot roam the earth and physical life without some sort of body or avatar. You have a human body, but consciousness can operate in life in many different ways; just think of all the animals and living things that exist in life: they're all conscious entities operating in physical life in some shape and form, like a bird or a tree.

To reiterate, in your physical being, in your body, you are limited to present-day reality, whereas you as a conscious being can experience time and space as much more expansive. You can literally revisit the past by entering your memories and construct a future, like a dream, to explore as well. Your body cannot enter these alternative realms of time but you, as consciousness, can.

When you meditate and enter your mind, you, as consciousness, are navigating away from the present moment as if to step back from the experience of your body and physical life, as if to step back from operating your body. Therefore, having a strong and healthy meditation position is important so you, as consciousness, can roam free in your mind (and beyond) without restriction.

When meditating, it is as if your body is on standby while consciousness travels the worlds within, just as your body can roam and travel the Earth, uncovering new places, learning new things, and unlocking new and enlightening experiences. You can choose to engage with your body at any moment during your meditation and return to, or awaken into, your experience of life, and this is what makes meditation so vastly different from sleep. All you have to do is place breath ahead of any experience that you want to get out of and detach from, and then open your eyes.

ENTERING THE MIND

When you have successfully locked into your meditation and have entered your mind, you can easily distinguish three key realms of awareness that you can easily venture into: present, past, and future and are like separate worlds of their own.

To roam in the present realm, just open your eyes, wake up your body, and continue to experience the world with your body. Consciousness is existing in its avatar to experience the present experience of creation. In meditation, whenever you sense anything from your physical senses—for example, if you hear or smell something—you, as consciousness, are closest to the present experience of life.

When consciousness ventures into and relives a memory, you, as consciousness, are entering another realm of awareness, the past. The deeper you venture into this realm, the further you navigate away from life and the present experience of creation. Consciousness is likely recreating an image of its avatar, your body, to experience the past or expired experiences of creation, although how you venture into your past is up to you; you can literally be a fly on the wall of your own memory if you wish or perhaps be an elephant in the room.

If something grips you down here, like a trauma or difficult memory, remember you are in full control always. Just breathe consciously and you will return closer to the present moment as you remind yourself that the memory is not life; it was life or rather a revived experience of life, but now it's an illusion that isn't real. Don't forget you are a creator witnessing creation so you can play around with details if you struggle to see its elusive nature.

The final realm of awareness, the future, though there is no particular order, is a little tricky to recognise because the future is a predetermined or pre-life state. We often think of the past as behind us and the future in front of us, and though this is correct for the experience of time and space with our bodies, to consciousness, it works a little differently.

To consciousness, the future is where it exists most of the time because whatever is on your mind, or your mindset, is often governing your experience of life and is determining your next physical move in the present. The future may indeed be ahead of your body, but in terms of consciousness, the future is just a creation in waiting. The future is a predetermined state which is brought into the present, just like an idea, a dream, or a vision of your future.

The next time you lock into your meditation begin identifying which realm of awareness you are in: Are you stuck in your senses and distracted by the happenings in the present? Are you venturing into the past and are living a memory? Or are you experiencing the future, a thought, or feeling that is trying to instruct you on what you should, could, or rather would be doing in life? Are you in your reality or an alternate reality?

ATTAINING STILLNESS

You must first be able to distinguish where you are in any given moment in your meditation; remember your body is in an idle position, and it is you, as consciousness, that is roaming the worlds within your mind. By being able to recognise where you are and exactly what it is you are experiencing, you can begin to distinguish yourself from any given experience in your mind.

Practising and exercising this ability trains your ability to detach and separate yourself from any given experience of life and to exist solely as consciousness. Existing solely as consciousness then enables you to just observe whatever your mind is presenting you instead of existing within, or gripped by, the experience itself. Meditating at this stage is to sit back in stillness and observe the creations of the mind; to observe creation from the creator's perspective.

Only once this ability is attained can you begin raising consciousness beyond the limitations of the creations or 'illusions' of the mind and into more transcendental states of being. I call this state of awareness *accepting Maya*. Maya is Sanskrit and it means illusion, divine creations, magic, and in some cultures, dark sorcery.

To accept Maya is to accept all the creations of the mind and body as illusions so you can recognise yourself as consciousness, an entity that is separate from any state of reality or being. This is so you can detach from creation and begin navigating yourself, as consciousness, to the source of all this creation, to the ultimate or supreme creator, to meet your maker so to speak, whoever or whatever you discover that to be.

CHAPTER 12

MOVING OUT OF THE MIND

This is where teaching meditation gets trickier because for consciousness to enter states of transcendence, consciousness must first enter the body of the soul. Already you have learned of a distinction between body and mind and that you exist solely as consciousness in both the experience of the body and in the experience of the mind. In this chapter, I'm going to attempt to explain how consciousness can move out of the mind and into your soul, a state of divine being detached from both mind and body.

The body allows you to be in and access the present experience of life, whereas the mind allows you to access the past and the future too. The past being all your memories and knowledge, the experiences that are no longer present; and the future being whatever state is predetermining your experience of life, an experience that can become present. The future, or pre-life state, can also be the experience of alternate realties like dreams, which are created experiences too.

In terms of observing the realms of the mind as creations, they go as follows:

- The present is a creation in action.
- The past is the end of or an expired creation.
- The future is a creation in waiting or new creation.

When meditating you can choose to venture into any of these realms to experience or observe them, and to detach, you need only to consciously breathe and raise awareness above them. However, if you are wanting to raise consciousness beyond the body and the mind, beyond any experience of physical and metaphysical life, then you are essentially embarking on a journey towards transcendence.

The journey into transcendence is a journey towards the sole creator or the beginning of all creation, whoever or whatever you discover that to be. And to do so, you need to enter your soul, which according to ancient Indian scriptures is a state equal to but isolated from the transcendent state like a drop of water out of an ocean.

EXERCISE

To help put this into perspective, get a piece of paper. The paper represents the source of creation, and if you tear off a small piece of the paper, that small piece would represent your soul.

BEGINNING THE TRANSCENDENTAL JOURNEY

The journey to the creator is what I call the transcendental journey, and it can feel like you are taking yourself, as consciousness, on an inner pilgrimage. To embark on the transcendental journey, you must first detach from any experience that the mind can present as real so you can locate a metaphorical portal.

This 'portal', as I have come to understand it, is theoretically where prana and consciousness entered on the day you were born, giving life to your body and enabling you to experience present day creation. Locating the portal can be likened to locating a black hole in the universe; it can be difficult. Also, everything about it can be the opposite to how you would imagine a black hole. Once located, the next task is for you, as consciousness, to enter it to make the journey backwards from creation to creator and visit the transcendent realm from which you came.

When you close your eyes and lock into your meditation, consciousness moves away from the experience of life in the body and enters the mind. If you imagine your mind like a room, a reality room if you will, where you as consciousness reside, it can put this theory into context and may help make locating the portal to transcendence a little more comprehendible.

When you enter your mind, your reality room, imagine that it is constructed and operates as follows:

In front of you is a pair of windows representing your eyes and all your physical senses.

- These windows are the windows into the present experience of life, and when you're awake you, as consciousness, are by this window and are operating your body. Think eyes open, windows open, eyes closed, windows closed. When your eyes are closed and you lock into your meditation, you are entering this reality room, the world of your mind.

To the right of you in your mind there is a door. This door leads into a library which houses all your memories and stores knowledge. Reliving a memory or accessing existing knowledge is like reading a book in this library.

- When you, as consciousness, venture down into this library you are heading into the past and the deeper you go, the further you venture away from the window, away from the present experience of life and deeper into your subconscious mind.

In the reality room itself, your mind, is where you construct reality: the future or predetermined state, an alternative reality, or a creation in waiting.

- Reality is merely a construct based on the data you retrieve from the library, your memories and knowledge, and the information being received through the windows from life and your physical senses.

If integrated, the reality that is constructed in your mind is then projected out onto your life through the window, determining your present experience of life and motivating your actions and how you proceed forward. It also illuminates the library, altering your perspective of the past.

- If you meditate regularly and exercise conscious control, you can learn to construct your own reality and create your own predetermined state. Or better yet, learn to experience life right at the physical senses without any predetermined value or experience and be fully immersed in the present.

Somewhere in this reality room is the portal where prana (life force) enters.

- Prana is what gives life to your body in the present; to the experiences of your past, reliving your memories; and to the reality constructed in your mind.
- Where consciousness ventures is where prana will follow and give life, allowing consciousness to have a conscious experience of it.
- You're in control always. So, ask yourself, what are you giving life to? Where are you guiding prana?

To locate the portal, focus on locating the source of your breath, prana, and detach from everything else in the present, past, and predetermined experiences of life. To detach from all creations, just breathe and reset your focus.

TIP!

When you close your eyes and begin control breathing, focus all your attention on your breath and use all your human intelligence to discover the source of this creation. Employ your senses to listen to and feel your breath. Employ your intellect, your knowledge, and raise questions to help you discover the source of your breath. Employ your creative abilities to help you construct and digest what you learn.

Returning to breath is to essentially restart your meditation, re-establish yourself as consciousness, and reset your focus on locating the source of your breath, the portal from which life enters. Once located, the aim is to enter the portal and begin your transcendental journey.

If at any moment during your meditation you get consumed by anything going on in your mind or body, you are attached and are gripped by an experience of creation. Consciousness is then only limited to the boundaries of whatever experience of creation it is consumed by, it's as if the experience you're attached to builds a wall around you to keep you from locating the portal.

When you realise that you are trapped by what's going on at the window in the present, something in the library in the past, or by the reality that has taken over your mind determining your future, just breathe consciously to detach from the experience. Control breathing sets you free from the bounds of these elusive experiences as if to carry you out of them and back on the path towards your transcendental journey.

Returning to breath also raises awareness of the experiences within. You can begin to map out the inner world that is your mind—as I have done with the reality room—and practising this regularly will enable you to get a good grasp on how your mind operates. You'll be able to quickly recognise when you are consumed by an experience of creation, what the experience is, and the elusive nature of the experience itself.

Venturing in and out of any experience within the mind is simply a matter of choice and only when you have realised and attained this ability, will you be able to develop the conscious precision required to locate and enter the portal. Transcendence aside, just exercising this ability can transform your experience of life, for you can pull yourself out of constructed realities which cause you inner conflict, for example, realities that make you feel anxious.

TIP!

Reality is merely a predetermined experience comprised of the past and present experiences of life. If the content in your past is not useful, navigate your body in the present to more useful experiences. Learn and experience new things so that you have more content to develop healthier predetermined states that govern your experience of life. Learning and experiencing new things is to basically live in the present and get out of being stuck in a troubled or unfulfilling past.

ENTERING THE PORTAL

Prana is like magic, and breath is like the pump that keeps the magic alive. Yoga is a practice that elongates the breath and strengthens the force of each inhale and exhale. When meditating, you are going to need your force of breath to carry consciousness into the portal, to counteract the force of prana coming through the portal as if to swim against a current.

To enter transcendence is to seek the creator, which means to enter a state of being that is beyond life, creation, itself. Entering the portal is naturally a challenge because you are essentially going against your way of being in life. Like a survival mechanism, your mind and body will do whatever it can to keep you from locating this portal because entering it suggests exiting life, hence why life encourages and creates attachments. 'Exiting life' does not mean death; death can only occur to your body. Entering the portal is consciousness, you, entering a state of deathlessness beyond life and death, or in other words, entering the body of the soul.

Where accepting Maya is the first level of awareness (accepting all experiences of the mind and body as creations or illusions), this second level of awareness (where you can recognise yourself as consciousness above all creations/illusions) is what I call realising *Atman*.

Atman is Sanskrit for soul or core consciousness and realising (not yet being) Atman is the moment you realise that there is something far greater than your experiences of life, and each time you meditate at this level of awareness, you are now aiming to discover your soul and enter a state of *Samadhi*, which is Sanskrit for union with the divine creator. Samadhi can be likened to the Buddhist philosophy of reaching Nirvana and reaching this ultimate state of awareness is the state of transcendence.

CHAPTER 13

MOVING INTO TRANSCENDENCE

Embarking on the transcendental journey is to essentially go on a pilgrimage, though this one occurs within. Like any pilgrimage, the transcendental journey comes with as many challenges as it will enlightening experiences. Based on all I have learned about meditation thus far and drawing inspiration from my own experiences, I have deconstructed the journey into three key levels of awareness:

1 Accepting Maya

Accepting all experience as creation/illusion to detach.

2 Realising Atman

Navigating consciousness into the soul for consciousness to realise itself as being.

3 Experiencing Samadhi

Transcendence, the experience of truth and union with the divine.

This is a journey that transcends life and can often take more than one meditation sitting to complete. Theoretically, depending on an individual's state in life, the transcendental journey can also take more than one lifetime to complete.

Raising consciousness into transcendence is about expanding the conscious field to reach Samadhi. Practising detachment pushes the boundaries of that field further out and explains why each meditation affiliated with the transcendental journey can feel like a continuation from the last as consciousness rises with each successful meditation.

In the five-step process, I introduced you to the practical steps of meditation so you could learn how to meditate and prepare your body for the transcendental journey, should you choose to embark on it someday. In the previous two chapters you learned how to deepen your meditation by recognising the elusive nature of reality and how attachment is designed to keep you from locating the portal into transcendence.

The transcendental journey is a personal one, and in addition to breathwork and technique, it will require dedication and perseverance to complete. Yoga is an invaluable practice for this process because it readies the body and mind to enter the transcendental state. If you have learned of the Buddha's story of enlightenment, you may realise that his journey into transcendence was not exactly all that graceful. He was just willing to die for it.

In short, the Buddha went from riches to rags and from rags to almost ruin. Willing to detach from all worldly desires to seek the truth of life, including the preservation of the body, the Buddha sat in meditation underneath a Bodhi tree refusing to awaken until the truth was realised. By way of this commitment, the Buddha, formally known as Siddhartha, transcended and whatever he had experienced in Nirvana was so enlightening that he felt encouraged to return to his body and awaken from his meditation to be of service to the world.

Understanding the Buddha's story is why yoga is essential to meditation. Transcendence can be quite an extreme commitment and not one I would recommend attempting without mindful preparation first. Perhaps the ancient Indians developed yoga as a safer way to enter the transcendental state without having to risk your life for it.

People have experienced Samadhi in many ways, such as near-death and other traumatic experiences, spirit-medicine journeys, giving birth and becoming a parent, creating art, and even performing. Regardless of how you enter, my advice would be to practise meditation and embark on the transcendental journey mindfully.

Meditation is by far the safest route because if at any moment you need to break from it, you can do so easily. If you have strengthened your practice enough to begin this journey, then you will have developed the control and conscious precision to awaken from your trance voluntarily.

LEVEL I—ACCEPTING MAYA

Maya: Illusion

Accepting Maya is what I identify as the first level of awareness in the transcendental journey. It is to accept all and any experience of life and reality as a creation, as an illusion so you can reject it and detach from it. This expands the conscious field beyond the limitations of the mind and allows consciousness to reach broader states of awareness.

Embarking on the transcendental journey does not often start easily, or too kindly for that matter. Accepting Maya is to essentially reject all you know, love, and appreciate as true, and to reject all and any experience of life, as you know it, as real. The aim is to unite with the creator, and to do so, you must release yourself from any attachment to creation.

In your mind, you will need to free yourself from the attachment to all the people you know and love. You will be required to release yourself from your identity, your memories, your desires, and your hopes and dreams. Let go of expectation too. This does not mean you forget; it means you leave them where they are until the only one left is breath, so you can raise consciousness into realms beyond life. As well as all the positive connections to life, accepting Maya also means to detach from the negative connections to life too, like your traumas, doubts, and fears. Let it all go.

When you have successfully detached from all material illusion, all that is left is breath, which sustains prana and consciousness itself.

LEVEL 2—REALISING ATMAN

Atman: Soul

The second level of awareness in the transcendental journey is to recognise yourself as consciousness and realise that there is a higher self, Atman, the body of the soul. At this level of awareness, it's all about making your way into the portal.

To visualise this state, imagine having detached from every experience of life—past, present, and future—and all that remains is you, consciousness, and your breath. You have expanded your conscious field beyond your mind and you're in a state of complete darkness and in isolation, sitting in a state of stillness surrounded by nothing. It is at this crucial point you can begin seeking the portal, which can be like a pinpoint of light like a very distant star in the night sky.

Your aim at this stage is to get closer to and eventually into the light. Ancient prophesies suggest that the portal will only be revealed to you when you are ready and deserving and could explain why many religions offer a specific way of being in life. Regardless, how you reach and enter this portal is something you must learn to do innately.

This is your transcendental journey, and though it may very well be the actions in your life which determine how bright the light shines through this metaphorical portal or it could be random in terms of accessibility, this is something for you to discover for yourself. I say take a chance and live your life your way, listen to your truth and let the truth be your guide to Samadhi.

LEVEL 3—EXPERIENCING SAMADHI

Samadhi: Transcendence

The experience of Samadhi at the final stage is reportedly an experience of oneness. It is to enter the portal and unite with the sole creator of all creation. It is here you realise the truth of life, death, and creation. Below is an excerpt from my meditation journal; as you read, please keep in mind that this is merely a personal experience and not a definitive example of what transcendence can be. Samadhi is more accurately experienced in tiers, and I presume that what I experienced was merely a tier of Samadhi, not the ultimate experience that one can attain.

I felt like I was standing on the decimal point of the numerical value of pi. I turned my head one way and I saw myself as a fully formed construct, a number three. My body, a finite structure sitting contently in meditation, was in a moment between life and death. I turned my head the other way, .141592653589 . . . and I could see into all of creation; I could see everything that is, that was, and that will be and can be of life and creation. There was neither an end nor a beginning; it was just ongoing, limitless. It went as far as my imagination could stretch. It was infinite.

While I wanted to jump into it, I couldn't, but I could look up, and what I was witnessing was a night sky of light filled with black imploding stars, each one alluring and enticing me to enter, calling me into a new place. A new world? A new adventure? A new body? Where was I supposed to go? What was in them? Was it death? Would I have ended up in an unknown place, in an alternate realm of time and space? I wondered if one of these stars would've taken me back home to my body.

As I stood there in awe contemplating my fate, I felt my body calling. 'Exhale', it whispered. 'Exhale'. It soon insisted and then, 'Exhale!' it commanded, and then I exhaled, and there I was, back in my flat and awakened by my body as if to wake up from a dream. I came to realise that I had entered this space with a full set of lungs, and my body had saved me from transcendence, but why? There is much to this mystery to solve, but I do know one thing for certain: I need to up my yoga.

3.14159265358979323846264338327950288419716939937510582
0974944592 . . .

There isn't too much more I can say about transcendence without sounding overly dogmatic and I hope what I have presented gave you a good idea of what the transcendental journey is and can be like. In the next section, I'm going to introduce you to an alternative way to kick-start your meditation practice prior to even sitting in contemplation, and offer an alternative way to awaken your potential without having to rely on transcendental states of awareness.

SECTION 4

INTEGRATIVE DEVELOPMENT

CHAPTER 14

ACTIVATING INTELLIGENCE

Meditating or trying to meditate can be a frustrating process if you're not used to it. Fortunately, before you attempt to sit in contemplation, detach from reality, and seek portals into enlightenment, there is a simpler way to begin your practice. You can activate an innate intelligence that is stored within your body. This innate intelligence I'm referring to is the knowledge that is

You may have learned that chakras are these pools of energy located at key points along the body. Originating in Vedic scriptures, chakra means wheel or disk. Each of these rotating disks, or whirling pools of energy, carry within them the knowledge of your life and truth. They start at the root, at your anus, and run along the body to the top of your head, at the crown.

There are seven chakras and the energy flows as follows, briefly speaking:

1. The root chakra, located at the anus, carries the knowledge of health.

2. The sacral chakra, located at the sex organ, carries the knowledge of well-being.

3. The solar plexus chakra, located at the navel, carries the knowledge of intuition and trust.

4. The heart chakra, located at the centre of the chest, carries the knowledge of desire and direction.

5. The throat chakra, located at the throat, carries the knowledge of truth and expression.

6. The third-eye chakra, located at the centre of the brain/mind, carries the knowledge of insight and wisdom.

7. The crown chakra, located at the top of the head, carries the knowledge of life and creation.

Your chakras get blocked if their values are neglected; therefore, to begin unblocking your chakras and activating the flow of energy from root to crown, you need to pay attention to them and act upon the knowledge which awakens you to your potential in life.

Activating your chakras isn't a difficult process; in fact, they're much more straightforward when approached logically. Starting at the root, you must realise and work through any conflicts in each chakra and restore equilibrium. I call this process integrative development.

Integrative development is about aligning your body and mind as one being so that who you are and how you feel on the inside is also true on the outside and vice versa. When there are no conflicts between mind and body you, consciousness, can detach from life's experiences and navigate into meditative states with much more ease and flow.

You can also use your integrative development as a process of integration after any life transforming experience, such as near-death experiences, traumatic experiences, and psychological breakthroughs. The chakras ensure your body is working optimally and in accordance to your truth, whatever you determine or discover your truth to be. As you develop, you will soon realise the power that you harness and what you're able to do with the body, the avatar that you have been given to experience life.

HOW TO MEDITATE ON EACH CHAKRA

As the chakras are associated with the body, the simplest way to utilise them in meditation is to focus on the area in need of development, observe the cause of the blockage, and then begin stimulating an energy of clearance. For instance, if you are dealing with sexual trauma, there will likely be a blockage or conflict in your sacral chakra, your well-being. Therefore, you would want to stimulate and develop the sacral energy to aid your healing. To stimulate a chakra in meditation, mantras and visualisations can help. You can use a mantra like an affirmation that verbally counteracts how you feel; for example, if you feel insecure, you can chant 'I am secure' repeatedly until you trust your mantra as true. Or you can visualise a secure presence in your mind and consciously raise awareness to the aspects or energies in your life that restrict this visualisation from manifesting and becoming a reality.

Trusting and restoring faith is just the first part; the second part is to act. In meditation you are essentially realising what you need to do in life to restore equilibrium in your chakra. Once you know what it is you must do, you must then do it—you must face the truth and act in accordance. If you trust you are secure, then be fearless; if you realise something is causing a restriction, lift the restriction.

Do not feel intimidated by this. Chakras work in a specific order so as you develop the sense and confidence to act mindfully, you will realise this order as you navigate through this section.

CHAKRAS IN OPERATION

Technically speaking, chakras are generators of electromagnetic fields which generate energy based on the instructions delivered by your reality, your predetermined state, the truth you set your mind to. When integrating awareness from your meditation you are charging your chakras, which is why it is always important to live and operate in accordance with your truth and positively charge your electromagnetic field.

Each chakra, each rotating disk, can be likened to a magnet rotating inside of a coil generating an electric current. The frequency of the current is what determines the size of your electromagnetic field. What determines the current is whatever signal your mind is sending your body. If you are operating in accordance with your truth, then your body will respond positively and generate a large magnetic field, repelling any external energy that does not serve your truth and attracting the energy that does. Your body will work like a magnet, how well is simply a matter of how true to life you are.

When you think of your ability to sense space and how you can sometimes sense specific energies around you, like sensing positive energy and negative energy, think of these sensations like your chakras generating an energy field of guidance. What your mind is set on, whatever instruction you are sending your body, your chakras will operate accordingly, which is why mantras and visualisations help. So, think about what you want from life and believe in it, make it true and your body will work to attract and guide your senses to it and you just have to trust. It is a neat way to think of your body working like this; it is like training your human superpowers, the power to manifest.

Each chakra works like a little mind, a miniature control centre that amalgamates a mini reality, each one instructing a key aspect of your body on how it should function based on the instruction it receives. When you integrate knowledge after your meditation, you are informing or tuning in your chakras to the frequency of your truth. Whereas, when you enter your meditation, your chakras inform consciousness of your experience of truth in life.

This is why your position and aligning your posture is an important step in meditation: so the energy to and from your chakras can flow with ease. When your posture is in alignment, each inhale will carry knowledge from root to crown to inform consciousness of the state of truth in life (physical truth). Each exhale will send knowledge from crown to root to inform your chakras of the state of truth beyond life (metaphysical truth). When all is balanced and equal, breathing keeps the cycle of truth in a constant state of flow. If your chakras are not balanced, the knowledge exchanged with each inhale and exhale is conflicted and thus creates conflict.

Chakras represent how your mind and body work together to create the life you want; however, how well they work together is determined by your acceptance of innate truth. For example, if you know that a certain food is bad for you but you eat it anyway, you go against the wisdom of your innate truth. This then causes a disconnect between body and mind as you override your natural response/instinct. Another example, if you know a certain relationship is toxic and you choose to remain in it anyway, you override your intuition and go against the inner response, creating conflict between inner and outer life.

Throughout this section, in each chapter, you will learn about each chakra's value and its allocated body part in a pre-enlightened state. You will also discover each chakra's elevated value and position post-enlightenment, and I will also share a corresponding step of a tantric meditation technique designed to stimulate each chakra.

The tantric meditation is like spiritual play and can evoke states of ecstasy. It is an advanced meditation practice, and with all I have learned about meditation, tantra has by far been the most tangible and exciting evidence of its benefits. Tantric meditation is not just about sex; it is about evoking spirit into the experience of life, and when you learn how to balance and utilise your chakras, you will be able to take command of your body and perform tantric meditations.

My first tantric meditation felt like an intense orgasmic climax at my chest. Unbeknownst to me at the time, I had apparently unlocked my heart chakra—which is said to carry the knowledge of your desires, the heart's desire. After experiencing what was such an intense inner orgasm, I felt encouraged to try it again. On my second attempt, I felt an orgasmic eruption at the top of my head, and what followed is what I describe as a showering rush of chemicals running down from my brain, through my body, and climaxing again at every nerve ending. It felt as if prana was piercing through my fingers and my toes. It was euphoric.

In an enlightened world, the notion that the body is a temple becomes quite an accurate comparison, especially when you realise what your body houses (Atman) and what your body can do (create life). If you struggle to connect with the concept of chakras, just think of the following chapters as steps in a personal development program designed to awaken your highest potential.

CHAPTER 15

START AT THE ROOT

TANTRIC MEDITATION
STEP 1. ACTIVATE YOUR ROOTS

Once in your meditation position, begin pulsating your pelvic
floor at one-second intervals to draw in life energy, like the roots
on a plant drawing up water from the soil.

The root chakra, located at your anus, represents your connection to life. Its primary service is to ensure that you are healthy and that your role in sustaining life is balanced. It helps you ensure that your contribution to earth is equal to what you consume from it.

To measure the wellness of this chakra, assess your stool. Think of it like this, can the waste that comes out of your body nourish the earth just as well as what you consume from the earth to nourish your body? This chakra is all about the physical preservation and connection to all life; it carries the knowledge of your state of health and according to ayurvedic yogic principles, assessing nutrition is the best place to start.

The root is your body's most important chakra because it teaches you about sustaining your life and staying physically healthy. Everything you consume has an impact on your body, and your body will tell you if a food is good or bad for you, which can be measured by your waste product. If you spend time adjusting your diet by paying attention to the health of your stool, you would be surprised at how well you can maintain a healthy and balanced inner-physical operation.

Food is fuel for the body and what we provide as waste is like fuel for the earth; therefore, it is so important to ensure that a balanced and sustainable cycle of giving and receiving nourishment is maintained. Furthermore, this is also how you can develop a strong immune system. It is no coincidence that in India, immune-boosting foods such as turmeric, garlic, and ginger have been a staple of their diet for millennia. The root also ensures that you are breathing correctly, as every inhale and exhale represents the same cyclical connection to all life on Earth like a circuit.

Without healthy roots, you cannot grow, and the chances of enlightenment will be significantly weakened. When you raise consciousness to this level of awareness within your body, you will stealthily train your senses to know what is good and bad for you. When you go to the supermarket, you should be able to tell the ripeness of a fruit or the nutritional benefit of a vegetable without question.

You live in an age whereby you have access to stored nutritional knowledge at your very fingertips, so you can develop the wellness of this energy centre conveniently and restore health quickly. If in doubt, you may wish to consult a nutritionist.

What is most brilliant about this chakra is that when you build a sustainable connection to all life, it can teach you where to settle down and set your roots. This becomes a physical decision as it requires little thinking and more responding because you are settling in accordance to the needs of your physical body. For example, moving to more fertile land and surrounding yourself with an abundance of resources, so that you can live your life with ease and comfort without threat to your existence. The root is an excellent source of knowledge that is not difficult to balance. As long as you pay attention to your health and physical development, this chakra will blossom and energy will flow from it with ease.

POST-ENLIGHTENMENT

Imagine being able to smell sickness, taste destruction, and hear toxicity in the air; this is what life may be like at the root level of awareness in an enlightened being. When you consider how easily you can tell the difference between a rotten piece of fruit and a healthy one using your senses today, a heightened health sense is not too far outside the realm of possibility.

Your ability to sense the health status of life raises in consciousness, and the root chakra is elevated from your anus to the base of your spine. When consciousness is raised, your senses are heightened, and you will be amazed at their potential to assess health when you are fully self-realised.

The root chakra also serves as a great platform to raise consciousness into even higher realms of awareness in meditation. Just how the deep roots of a tree enable it to stand tall and grow closer to the stars, a deep connection to life will enable you to reach higher states of transcendence.

Furthermore, if your relationship with life is healthy and abundant, you will less likely want to cut away from your roots. Your roots keep you safe and grounded, and a healthy root chakra will keep you feeling secure during spiritual play such as the tantric meditations. They also ensure that you do not push your body beyond what it can handle when sitting through lengthier meditations.

The information that comes through your root chakra also carries with it the information about the state of life on Earth. This will aid the development of your creations to ensure the preservation of life and life's evolutionary journey through the cosmos.

Maintaining a healthy root chakra can even help restore and benefit your karma. Think of karma like a spiritual resource centre, like a bank of energy that can help you create the life you need. Karma helps to ensure that you stay on the truest path in life, such as making signs of opportunity easily noticed and inner guidance easily trusted. Good karma ensures you are living blissfully, and good karma starts at the root, your connection to life.

A compassionate value of a balanced root chakra is your ability to sense the status of health in other beings in life too. Wouldn't you like to live in a world where all beings work to keep each other healthy and alive, simply because of sustainability and the preservation of life? Sustaining the evolutionary development of the conscious collective is good practice for our roots are all connected.

Just by breathing, you provide valued sustenance to life on Earth, so if you are not healthy, the prana you provide is weakened. Life will always favour preservation over destruction. Therefore, if you are consciously contributing to its preservation, life will consciously return the favour and will make living your life easier. In summary, respect and nurture your roots to ensure a healthy and balanced life.

CHAPTER 16

LEARN HOW TO PLAY

TANTRIC MEDITATION
STEP 2. STIMULATE YOUR SACRAL

Begin pulsating your pelvic floor at double the speed,
as if you draw in life energy up from the root and
deeper into the body.

The sacral chakra, located at your sex organ, is all about your interactions with life. Where the root focuses on inner-physical well-being, the sacral chakra focuses on your outer physical well-being. If you think about the world as one large playground, this chakra teaches you how to play healthily within it. Everything from your physical fitness through to your sexual expression, this chakra encourages activity and play.

Once you have figured out how to keep your body healthy (the root), it is time to learn what you can do with it. It is connected to your sex organ because primitively speaking, this is how you can tell when something is pleasurable or not. Your sex organ is like your physical truth-teller; however, as an advanced conscious being, you will also feel physical sensations across the entire body. Like the blood rushing to your face when you blush, and the hairs on your arms and legs standing erect when you experience shock. The sacral centre provides you with outer guidance by responding to the world around you.

This chakra focuses on reducing pain and increasing pleasure. If neglected, pain will increase, and if overused, pleasure sensations will begin to numb. Therefore, it is important to maintain balance at this energy centre. A general rule with this chakra, and indeed your body, is to use it before you lose it, but if you abuse it, it will fail.

Having an active and healthy sex life is a great way to exercise and engage this chakra, but good flexibility and mobility are equally as important when contributing to the health of this chakra. Focus on the fluid movement of the hips and the flexibility of the spine to guide the development of your sacral energy. Your body is for you to use, it is for you to create with, to experience life with, and to absolutely express yourself with. Enjoy it and exercise its ability.

This chakra encourages you to investigate your physical curiosities, everything from what is hiding under a rock to what could be lurking on top of a mountain. You just need to ensure you are fit enough to explore. The world is waiting for you to discover it and the sacral energy is stimulated when you learn and play.

Healthy sacral energy aims to maximise physical potential, such as improving physical fitness and endurance so that you can indeed play. It will also teach you about the people you want to connect with, the community you can contribute to, and the tribes that you can be a part of. Think in terms of movement and moving with others who like to move to the same rhythm of life as you.

Furthermore, if everyone on this planet were able to develop their sacral energies without shame, then saying no to things that you do not want to play or interact with would likely become a lot easier. There would also be much more respect for your own body and for the bodies of others.

Physical connection will amount to much more than just physical intimacy; it will make room for physical exploration and the discovery of truth in other beings and creations. It is not all about sex, this energy centre is about realising how other life-forms work, just as much as learning about how your own life-form works so all life can physically work together to preserve life.

POST-ENLIGHTENMENT

Elevated to the sacrum, this chakra evolves from the enjoyment of life to the creation and contribution to life. It elevates your contribution to the preservation of peace and harmony in life so all beings can play and create freely. It can also stimulate the motivation to procreate or not, depending on the state of play on Earth.

It can help you recognise your physical potential as a contributor and a creator of experience. From invention through to art, this energy centre raises consciousness of movement for play to movement for creation. Sex evolves to making love, pleasure evolves to ecstasy, and production evolves to passion.

Also, imagine having full command over your sexual organ and making sexual dysfunction a thing of the past. Everything is true in a post-enlightenment world, so you no longer need a truth-teller to provide guidance, which may also encourage abstinence too in times of spiritual devotion.

This chakra is probably where you realise how crucial living true to yourself is, prior to your transcendental experience. You will not need to change much about your life if you were living true to your nature before enlightenment. However, if this chakra is out of balance beforehand, life will feel like a complete transformation post-enlightenment, and quite possibly the reason why so many individuals seem to change their lives so drastically after transcendental experiences.

Do yourself a great favour and start exploring your truth and discover the world through your curiosities today, instead of waiting for tomorrow. As you do, note that you must ensure that you do not cause harm to self or to others, so that your karma continues to grow and serve the life you want to create.

With regards to your senses, you will be able to recognise a competitor for sports, an apprentice to mentor, a lover for sex, a teacher for enlightenment, and knowing how to successfully accomplish physical challenges. Again, it sounds like the content of myth, but if you think about physical attraction today, imagine what that would be like when consciousness is raised, and you can see the truth in everything. Additionally, you may notice that sex becomes a union of souls, procreation becomes a contribution to life, and the entire playground that is Earth becomes your home.

Post-enlightenment, this chakra can make you feel physically powerful and almost superhuman. It can make you realise the errors in your physical development and can encourage you to sustain peak physical fitness. It can ensure your body can serve whatever creation you need to manifest.

It can also make you realise the physical force of energy that you are, like an elephant aware of its stature. Finally, keeping this chakra balanced keeps you physically responsible, safe, and out of harm's way. It is certainly valuable knowledge to be aware of, for it sustains trust and an appreciation for all life in creation, your own included.

CHAPTER 17

TRUST YOUR GUT

TANTRIC MEDITATION
STEP 3. FILL UP YOUR GUT

Begin pulsating your pelvic floor but hold onto the pulse for longer intervals, as if you are drawing in life energy up from the root, through the sacral, and into the solar plexus chakra. Imagine that there is a cauldron located at your gut and each time you hold onto a pulse, you are filling up this cauldron with physical energy.

First positioned at your navel, the solar plexus is where you develop self-trust and its purpose is to ensure you use your finite experience on Earth wisely. When you know how to truly take care of yourself and you know what it is you can and cannot do with your body, energy flows into this chakra and is ready to be developed. It guides instinct and intuition and balancing this chakra provides you with independence, for you learn to only place your trust in the things that you need and are serving your truth.

With regards to generating electromagnetic fields, this chakra is the one that would be felt more potently within. Think of the terms *gut instinct* or *trusting your gut*. This chakra learns from the previous two, and how much you trust yourself is based on how well you can take care of yourself and how well you have learned to use your body.

This centre of knowledge in its pre-enlightenment role teaches you how to keep physical life operating smoothly. Therefore, if you do not know how to take care of your physical health or do not feel in ownership of your body, then trusting yourself becomes challenging and this chakra can only sustain the weak operation that is currently in place.

It helps to think of this chakra like a second brain that uses the knowledge within your physical body to serve the life you are preserving. You need to keep the brain fed with clean, sustainable, and healthy knowledge to feel motivated, productive, energised, and engaged. Your inner-physical sensations are programmed from here, everything from knowing when to eat to who to trust is felt at this critical point in your body.

It is like feeling when a situation is bad for you because of the sensations in the gut, such as feeling nauseated because of stress. Where the root and sacral chakras have external indicators, the solar plexus is internal as its role is connected to your internal organs.

Developing this chakra starts with the fulfilment of the previous two. So long as you are breathing and excreting healthily, and you are existing in and interacting with the world comfortably, you will learn how to train and raise this chakra's potential to serve you. All that is required is for you to listen and respond accordingly.

If, for example, you find yourself gaining excessive weight, feeling obsessed with how you appear in the world, and/or are constantly anxious, then this can be an indication of a problem somewhere in your root or sacral energies. Keep it simple: when you face self-doubt and you lack self-trust, scale back to the basics of life's operations, and focus on fulfilling your more basic needs.

Keep your root and sacral energies in harmony and support their operations, then you will trust what it is you must do to resolve conflict in life and restore equilibrium. When balanced, the solar plexus chakra ensures that you are always ready to launch into action for whatever life brings, or whatever you are bringing to life.

Think in terms of restoration and development, the solar plexus ensures you sustain a healthy way of being and grow in accordance with your truth. In summary, the solar plexus helps you become responsible and ensures that your life is running smoothly. It helps you sense time and space, assesses fight-or-flight responses, and determines if you can successfully accomplish something or not.

POST-ENLIGHTENMENT

When enlightened, this chakra elevates above the navel and is felt at the solar plexus as a source and a distribution of energy. The solar plexus is the epicentre of your physical body and raising consciousness within it, then places you at this governing epicentre of your body.

Sustainability is sensibility as life is now centred around the present experience and serving the needs of preservation. The needs of the body are easily satisfied and controlled which makes enduring physical demands much more tolerable. For example, rather than being focused on the difficulty of a task, you will carry out the task of learning how to make it less enduring.

The solar plexus also serves a tantric level and advanced meditation practices. Think of this second brain as housing crucial information that can help prepare the body for transcendence with great accuracy, knowing how much energy to store for your meditation and what physical preparations will be required for specific spiritual rituals and meditation practices.

Furthermore, your ability to trust in what you cannot see, touch, taste, smell, and hear is aided by this crucial chakra. When the crown chakra (the final/seventh chakra) is open, the solar plexus can also store metaphysical energy or knowledge that you receive from states of transcendence.

Think of this chakra, this second brain, as a backup store of divine knowledge when Maya seems to be working against you, for when you may experience failure and defeat for example. Ultimately, this chakra helps you trust in your way of being, and one you must develop should you want to focus on developing sustainable solutions to your life's problems.

CHAPTER 18

RAISE YOUR PRESENCE

TANTRIC MEDITATION
STEP 4. OPEN YOUR HEART

Once the gut is full, stop pulsating your pelvic floor and engage breath of fire to invigorate your body and pump energy up to the heart. To engage the breath of fire, known as Kapalbhati in yoga, begin pumping the stomach to breathe but only focus on a short and forceful exhale, let the inhale and the stomach inflate automatically. Imagine that the stem of a lotus flower is germinating out of this cauldron at the gut that is full of earth energy. Treat breath of fire as if it is stimulating the life of a lotus to germinate and grow inside of you

Once sustainable physical function from root to the gut is attained, your heart can then function optimally and pump in accordance to your body's needs and demands, as well as your mind's wants and desires. Think of your heartbeat pulsating a frequency that radiates and raises your outer electromagnetic field so you can attract what you truly want from life and repel all that does not align with your truth. If your heart is beating to a false rhythm, then you are expressing a false truth, hence why energy and knowledge from the first three chakras need to flow into and instruct your heart centre.

If you imagine the whole world existing in silence and darkness and all you can hear is the beating of other's hearts in order to communicate and sense each other's presence in life, it may help you understand the power and importance of this chakra. Your heart is like its own form of communication and is designed to raise your presence in life so that you can attract energy such as opportunity, knowledge, and love.

The heart is the closest thing to having a superhuman ability and to train it and harness control over it, you must first look after it. By consciously taking care of your heart's health, you are essentially showing love and appreciation to your own life and body. It is incredibly important that you are aware of this, especially if you are seeking love in life. How well you take care of yourself will determine the types of energies you will attract, or in other words, how much love and appreciation you show for your life will echo how much love and appreciation life should offer you in return.

Your heart needs to be fully open for love to be abundantly exchanged. If you think of love simply as truth, then it can teach you how to use your heart. For love to manifest, your truth must first be recognised and accepted, which means accepting yourself and being able to express your truth unapologetically so others can accept you for your truth too. Love cannot exist if the truth has to be compromised. Even if your expression of truth is inaccurate or poorly communicated, an open heart will attract teachers and gurus to enlighten you. This is the beauty of expression and the magic of the heart and its electromagnetic field.

It is so important to fulfil and balance the previous three energy centres because your truth of life will at least be derived from experiences that you can trust. When the root, sacral, and solar plexus energy centres are satisfied, you will have enlightening insight into the person that you are, which then allows the heart to express this energetically, almost like subliminal communication.

When the heart chakra is balanced, it makes you feel that you belong in life without question, because you are existing optimally within it. After all, by this point, you would have figured out the fundamentals on how to survive (the root), how to grow (the sacral), and what choices to make (the solar plexus).

The heart chakra is what makes your life thrive and is where you begin to realise how much contribution to life you can make. It encourages you to follow where your senses want to go; for example, if you smell something baking that you must try or you hear a sound that makes you want to dance, this is your heart chakra in action.

Think about the people who you find inspiring, notice their fearless nature and their willingness to live and fight for life. Your heart inspires and seeks inspiration, it can heal and be healed, and it can love and be loved, and so on. Where the first three chakras are more in service to you, the heart opens you up to be in service to life, just by living and being completely you. The heart is where you shine, and it is how you are truly seen.

POST-ENLIGHTENMENT

What truth would you love to experience in the world? What experience of truth can you bring into the world to love? This is the elevation of the heart chakra. It relocates to the centre of your chest after enlightenment, uniting your mind and body. It is about contributing to a better world and embracing others, and the heart chakra can provide you with the ability to do so easily and freely when consciousness is raised within it.

Imagine being able to consciously connect with a lost love or communicate your presence to energy on the other side of the planet. Imagine being able to transform the weather, impact world events, and prevent natural disasters simply by raising your heart's magnetic field. Though you might not be able to affect drastic change in the world on your own, the heart teaches you how you can communicate and work together with others to achieve such great results.

The will of the heart is said to have the power to raise and destroy armies, and you do not have to look too far back in history to realise it. People today will fight wars for the love of their country, for their leaders and rulers, and for their families and loved ones, so do not underestimate the power of the heart.

When you think about the remarkable things that people will do for love, you realise what the heart chakra can achieve when it is operating at its full potential. The heart centre is the centre of the action, it inspires, it leads, and it encourages you to exist with purpose and value. You have a body you can use and a dream that you can manifest, and it is at the heart where action and desire meet to provide direction.

What is most fascinating about the heart centre is that it can communicate. Just as much as you can raise your presence and send a signal, you can receive the signal of a presence too. For instance, sensing when a loved one on the other side of the world is in trouble.

You can sense electromagnetic pulses or frequencies around you. When you can raise consciousness to send and receive knowledge like radio frequencies, you can then effectively communicate energy and connect compassionately with all life in creation. If you have ever been in love, then you may have noticed you tend to sense love in everything, nothing is too troubling or burdening, and love truly becomes all you need.

Ultimately, the heart represents the intentional operation of your life because it serves to align your body and mind in accordance with the truth of your soul. If your body and your mind are serving different truths, then your heart will operate in conflict and you will manifest desires that will fail to fulfil you completely.

The heart is where the mind and body meet, where physical and metaphysical energy connects, and is why you begin developing at the root. The body is vulnerable to death; therefore, the chakra system is designed in such a way to ensure the body's preservation needs are satisfied first. This is so that when you become enlightened, you learn to only integrate and express the truth of what the body, what life, can handle.

CHAPTER 19

BE HONEST

TANTRIC MEDITATION
STEP 5. STIMULATE YOUR TRUTH

Engage your control breath and let the sensations in your body settle. Once settled, begin humming or chanting your mantra or you can chant 'aum' or 'om'—known as the frequency of creation. Stir a vibrational frequency by starting the vibration inside your gut 'aaa', through your chest and throat 'uuu', and into and out of your head 'mmm'. Hum or chant as if to grow the lotus stem up your body and

The throat chakra is the force of creational frequency and the vibrations of truth. Just like when a baby cries out when it needs something, and the parent serves the baby's need, this chakra works quite similarly to that. Whatever truth you express in life, life will serve you accordingly. Thus, to balance this chakra, you need only to start being honest.

Whatever you express in life represents your truth, and if you are expressing lies then you will be met with more illusions and life will struggle to represent a true and fulfilling experience. You may also find yourself raising more questions about life and doubting your experience if not living true. What you express sends a vibrational force into life so that life can respond accordingly; for example, if you are constantly expressing what you need, the chances of that need being fulfilled in some form or fashion are significantly greater.

Expressing your truth does not necessarily mean having to speak it, especially if you struggle to communicate with words. Expressions through art, dance, study, and play are all examples that are equally as valuable. Present your truth to the world in the best way you know how. So long as you are actively being true in life and the force of the frequency can be felt, your truth can easily manifest. Even entrepreneurial pursuits and activism are expressions of truth, anything you do in life that is true engages your throat chakra because you are ready to enlighten others or be enlightened should your truth come into question.

If you find it difficult to express yourself, then start expressing yourself in meditation; for example, you can scream as loud as you want inside your mind and nobody can hear you. Learn to get comfortable with your own truths and start speaking them. Also, get comfortable creating realities around your truths inside your mind, and eventually, you will develop the sense to externalise your truth and present it to life.

Once you evolve your truth into a vibrational force, a physical expression that others can witness and experience too, you will begin to build a life centred around truth, without fear, and without judgment or hate. This chakra is all about eliminating vulnerability and strengthening your stance in life. When truth filters out of the heart, life is no longer a mystery, and neither are you.

Where the heart informs life that you exist and are present, the truth notifies life as to why, and this is how life can learn to respond and serve you accordingly. Being present without truth is to simply exist as Maya, whereas being present with truth is to exist as truth within Maya. Operating by your truth charges your electromagnetic field to attract truth and repel illusion, which in a world that does not always command the truth can make you an unpopular person to some and an enlightening person to others.

Learn to sit and be comfortable with your truth in meditation so you can recognise and accept it in life. The truth is extremely important because you do not want to be raising the energy of illusion and attracting untrue entities to your life. This will only invite destruction and chaos, and you may find yourself raising and entering conflict.

If you want life to swing in your favour, then, just as you did when you were a baby, speak up and be heard so that life has an opportunity to respond. If life does not, then grow your truth and raise your vibrational frequency even louder so you can be heard from energies afar. Explore different modes of communication, styles of expression, and connecting with different energies outside of your zone of comfort. Do not confuse this with simply raising your voice, think more in terms of raising your determination and intention to live your life your way.

The truth will make life a lot less grey, your life is clear and who you are and what you stand for will become expansive and difficult to destabilise. This is not to say you will become stubborn and rigid; it means you will grow in alignment with truth and evolve accordingly. The higher you grow, the more deeply you become rooted, like a tall tree with sturdy roots in a blossoming forest.

When you live your life exercising your truth, you will train your senses to respond to and seek the truth too, which can make sailing through life a breeze. You will know not to assert yourself into places where your truth is not welcome, though, simply by existing as truth you may inspire those around you to question and check in with theirs.

It is not about existing as the truth, it is about expressing a truth, your truth, and if all people expressed their individual truths, then maybe the world would represent the universal truth a little more clearly. Perhaps that is the point of it all: to create a world that feels like and represents the experience of Samadhi. After all, if there is a single creator, then each being on this plane of existence represents an individual piece of it. Each one of us is just a piece of truth ready to enlighten the world a little more.

POST-ENLIGHTENMENT

Truth elevates from expression to reception as you become more of an antenna for truth and communicate from higher realms of awareness. In life, you will find yourself to be a preserver of truth, however unpopular that may make you. The truth chakra elevates from your throat to the top of your spine.

In kundalini and kriya yoga, it is at this point the energy of life has coiled up your spine like a snake, carrying with it the knowledge of life from your root through to your truth, ready to clasp onto your brain stem and ignite your third eye. Once life is a true experience, you can carry this knowledge into your mind and begin to resolve inner conflict. It is at this point you are truly prepared for an enlightening experience in meditation. As you have a controlled breath to engage your control state, you now also have a control truth to measure all illusions against.

Being able to identify what is true enables you to recognise it, which makes it easy to detach from experience and enter states of transcendence with trust. In the Christian faith, it is said that if you follow the Ten Commandments, you will get into heaven. In Hinduism, it is said that if you live a good life, you will be reincarnated again as a human, as an advanced/evolved species. Both interpretations are suggesting that if you live a life that is true, you will be granted access to states of transcendence.

Religions, it seems, are trying to suggest how to be true; however, when you study their origin stories a little more closely, you realise that the truth is for you to locate and choose independently from within. Adam had a choice to eat the apple and Arjuna had a choice to fight in battle, either character from these religions had the option to operate true to their nature or be swayed by an external force. When you have realised your truth, choosing your path forward is clear and the uncertainty of what not to do becomes enlightened.

CHAPTER 20

WITHOUT JUDGMENT

TANTRIC MEDITATION
STEP 6. ACTIVATE YOUR TRUTH

Engage your control breath and lock into your meditation. Breathe deeply and use your stomach like a large pump. Use the force of life to open the bud of the lotus as if to open your third eye and encourage the flower to blossom. The sensation may feel something like filling up a water balloon at the top of your head, pumping water into it until

Once life is a true experience, consciousness can carry this wisdom and knowledge of truth through to all realms of awareness. For instance, if you are an individual who lives with childhood trauma, you can assess your trauma against your present experience of truth. You can begin inner healing as you uncover how much of your past was indeed a true experience of life, or a circumstance or consequence of an illusion. This is how you activate your third-eye chakra, pre-enlightenment. From the root, you grow in truth and learn in response to the innate wisdom stored in your body.

Your third eye is only concerned with seeking and restoring truth, and your development up until this point is basically teaching you how to live true to your nature, at all levels of physical existence and ability. If you fall away from your truth at any level, you will likely feel it in your body, signalling you to restore it before having to raise the conflict in your mind and meditation. There is no room or time for judgment, of self or upon others, as life at this level of operation is about resolution and the discovery of truth.

Your third-eye chakra is the sense of truth. If you have been living your life dishonestly, your third-eye chakra will struggle to balance and operate in full service. It will struggle to accept your innate wisdom as truth. For example, if you have convinced yourself that you are not hungry even though you are, you cause inner conflict between your body and mind. Or when you tell a lie and you negatively charge your magnetic energy, repelling the truth and denying the opportunity to become enlightened by life, you cause a conflict between consciousness and life.

By this point in your integrative development, you are fulfilling your life's demands without question or concern. You are healthy, you feel secure, you have trust, your heart is open, and your truth is expressed and now it is time to assess your experience of life without judgment and learn of your truest nature.

In 1943, psychologist Abraham Maslow released *A Theory of Human Motivation*. In his paper, Maslow identifies a hierarchy of needs which suggests that humans must satisfy and fulfil a certain level of needs before feeling motivated to progress onto the next level. For example, a human must fulfil their basic physiological needs such as food, water, shelter, and warmth before feeling motivated to seek safety and security.

Once a human feels safe and secure, they are then motivated to fulfil their needs for love and belonging and so on. Maslow's hierarchy of needs works almost in parallel alongside this ancient Vedic construct of chakras. What Maslow identifies as self-actualisation can be likened to the state of being at the third-eye level before the experience of transcendence.

Self-actualisation represents the highest state of psychological development, where an individual's full potential is fully recognised.

Maslow identifies self-actualisation as the desire to know and understand, which conveniently sums up the pre-enlightenment role of the third eye.

Up until this point in your integrative development, life has been lived in response to, and in accordance with, inner or outer stimulus, such as the state of your health and your personal curiosities. When the third eye is in operation, you will begin seeking to explore higher intent. For example, questioning your intentions and developing the curiosity to learn the meaning of life. By this point in your development, you are seeking the truth of life itself, of all life. You are seeking a creator, life is not getting in the way, and it is where deep states of meditation begin.

As life these days does not unfold as straightforwardly as developing from root to crown, meditating from the third-eye perspective can be a great way to start assessing your life for fulfilment. For instance, you can assess how your roots may have gotten infected and why you are feeling self-destructive. Why you may have struggled to play happily on the playground and struggle to build healthy relationships. Why you may have struggled to trust yourself and develop independence. How you may have learned to close your heart and lower your presence in life. Why you may have found it difficult to express yourself honestly and ultimately check in with and reveal what your truth is.

Restore your life's journey and start assessing your attachments from the beginning and restore equilibrium from root to crown. A true meditation practice certainly begins with the development of a true life, and when you put this much conscious intent into your personal development, life begins to unfold like a meditation. You will learn to develop solutions, resolve conflict, realise truths, restore balance, and recover your health mindfully.

Furthermore, when operating from the creator's eye, you can easily step in and out of your experience of living in a conscious dance. You can move from a subjective experience of life and into an objective one whenever you feel off or out of sync. This can also help you when engaging in conversation and listening to others, when learning something new, and can help you improve focus and concentration for you are consciously engaged in maintaining balance in all aspects of life, relationships included.

The knock-on effects of maintaining balance actively reduce inner conflict and outer bias. You are sooner able to forgive yourself and others because you are actively engaged in self-sustainability and the preservation of life. Empathy, understanding, and the restoration of peace become sensible ways of being, and there is no need for life to cause any contention. The sooner restrictions are lifted and conflicts are resolved, the sooner you can get back to living life and learning from its experience.

Once life is balanced and true you can begin your journey into transcendence with a lot of ease. Your third eye is ready to navigate in and out of any experience in life, death, or creation without fear. For you have established the self-trust to preserve, destroy, or (re)create any experience in life should anything you experience during your transcendental journey throw you off balance.

POST-ENLIGHTENMENT

Life with an activated third eye is a life of complete truth. Truth becomes undeniable because it is everywhere and in everything. You can see through the illusion, through any creation, and directly into the truth, the creator. The third eye is open and in operation; therefore, you have attained the awareness to see a creator in every creation.

The ability to sense truth is practically instantaneous. Where you may struggle, however, is in places where you lack the subconscious context or knowledge to communicate the truth you feel. This is when you would sit in meditation and learn of ways to obtain and communicate knowledge. For example, perhaps you need to explore the laws of physics and chemistry to study and express a theory that you want to raise about the universe. You would then carry what you have studied into your meditation to see if the context fits and utilise your newfound knowledge to help you qualify and communicate the truth you feel.

This is what I refer to as manifesting the truth as fact, because sometimes what we feel or experience to be true can be difficult for others to comprehend unless backed up by evidence that satisfies the senses. If you think of all the different creation stories in the world, though similar in structure, the details are vividly different. All anyone has is whatever context they have to describe a truth, which is why I appreciate the language of math for it is truly universal and the closest thing humans have to unlocking the secrets of the universe.

What is liberating about the third eye being open is that you can carry consciousness into much deeper realms of awareness. You can detach from experiences with ease and enter states of transcendence at will. You can access the knowledge of a past life and explore the potential of a future one. This again sounds like the content of myth, but when you consider how deep your subconscious mind can go and the biological data you are born with that drives your biological functions, discovering how you developed such innate knowledge is only a detachment or two away at this stage of awareness.

Just imagine what you could achieve if you could access the knowledge stored in your conscious history and imagine having a hand in navigating your conscious evolution. The term wizardry certainly comes to mind whenever discussing the third eye. Imagine what advancements can be achieved in machine learning and artificial intelligence if such awareness could be engineered and applied to computer science.

It is also worth noting an additional role of the third eye, post-enlightenment, and the beauty of the third-eye chakra in this intelligent design. The third eye questions everything, even the value of enlightenment in life; therefore, it plays a significant role in keeping you consciously balanced throughout any conscious experience. As you delve into realms of awareness that are beyond your experience of life, from dreams, past life regression, and future manifestations, the third eye will enable you to remain in conscious control. Should ever any version or experience of Maya take you away from your experience of life, the third eye can bring you back. Theoretically speaking, it is training and engaging this chakra that can bring you back from psychosis and potentially prevent Alzheimer's.

CHAPTER 21

ACCESS TO KNOWLEDGE

TANTRIC MEDITATION
STEP 7. BLOSSOM

Engage your control breath to keep the flow of energy in motion, keep the lotus flower upon your head in bloom and the petals ever unfolding. If at any point during this meditation you feel the connection/sensation fading, repeat steps 1 – 7 and reopen the crown

Sir Francis Bacon, English philosopher and father of empiricism, coined the phrase *knowledge is power*, which makes the name of this final chakra an accurate translation. The crown chakra, located at the top of your head, represents your access to knowledge. Pre-enlightenment knowledge comes from the past, present, or future realms of awareness. Post-enlightenment, access to transcendent states and deep realms of awareness becomes available.

In a pre-enlightened state, this chakra is all about the facts of life: seeking fact, knowing a fact, and manifesting truth as fact. There is no room for any deniable truth, which is why the full potential of this chakra is only realised post-enlightenment. The crown focuses on solutions centred around preservation, destruction, or creation; however, how you apply this knowledge is at the mercy of what you know and your experiences in life. The crown is a powerful force and operating with an open crown chakra, without firmly planting your roots first, can make for quite a conflicting life experience. Sometimes the terms *mad scientist* and *evil genius* come to mind.

Without balancing the previous chakras, the crown will keep the mind active, stimulating energy that the body cannot contain, integrate, or handle. It can be quite a maddening experience because the body cannot keep up or function in accordance with the knowledge that is being developed. Life can feel reductive and if the crown opens up as a result of a traumatic experience in life, whereby consciousness has unconsciously transcended to remove itself from the trauma, then self-destructive habits can begin to form. The mind will struggle to settle as there is knowledge residing within that is active yet without context. Therefore, it is important to begin balancing at the root and work back up to transcendence if meditation and sitting with the mind are too troubling.

Life at the crown level of awareness prior to enlightenment can also make communicating a struggle, as the crown seeks to provide knowledge that serves the preservation of life. However, if you are unsure as to why you are preserving life, or if life isn't a true experience, the motivation to preserve is conflicted with the reality of the experience. Individuals who live with an open crown, pre-enlightenment, are highly intelligent but lack the intelligence to utilise their intellect for preservation, like an unhealthy doctor for example.

On the plus side, the crown represents the removal of obstacles and you will find yourself more focused on developing solutions, no longer debating the value of a problem. As far as the crown is concerned, where there is a problem, there is a solution to be found and the supposed formulas are simple: for present problems you seek solutions that preserve life. If there is a problem in the past, aka death, the solution is to destroy or detach for it no longer exists; and if there is a problem in the future, aka deathlessness/creation, then the solution is to create.

The force of energy that you can bring into life with your crown chakra open can be intimidating to others, so tread wisely and navigate through life as if you have the presence of an elephant. At times you may feel compelled to charge at full force and destroy illusions/ignorance in an instant, causing pain and chaos. Therefore, it is wise to keep in mind the force of a charging elephant, and the destruction that can ensue when operating at full intellectual force.

The crown, when open, connects you to the impact of planetary alignment and lunar and solar rotations can affect your body and conscious operation. If you are living life with your crown chakra open, then spend time noting how you feel during different days and seasons and raise self-awareness. Potentially, studying a person's crown chakra could provide insight into the behaviours of their mental health disorder, specifically schizophrenia and bipolar disorder.

If you think of the crown chakra like a hole at the top of your head that dilates and contracts to cosmic energy, like your pupils do to light, it could help you raise awareness enough to independently manage your mental health, which in theory could be quite effective for those who suffer from acute paranoia. Again, most of this will require further research in order for it to be applied to real life; however, the knowledge can be useful in developing your meditation practice.

Life with a balanced crown chakra can make life an enlightening experience, though you must be firmly rooted first. Everything you do has an intention and you are no longer troubled by your problems for you carry the knowledge of preservation, destruction, and creation and can consciously apply this knowledge accordingly. Meaning you know what to do to fulfil your dharma, your role in the preservation of life.

Dharma is Sanskrit for your true way of being or way of life, which becomes very apparent when your crown chakra starts to blossom. By this point in your development, you will have already realised what you are capable of in life, and there is little to almost nothing that can make you doubt it. You are at your highest level of potential that you can be prior to enlightenment. You have unlocked such awareness so innately that validation and self-doubt are unnecessary, and the only obstacle left to overcome is the access to transcendence. It is an obstacle because in order to detach, you will be required to question everything you have learned to trust.

POST-ENLIGHTENMENT

When enlightenment is fully attained it is said that your crown blossoms open like a lotus flower, and you have attained a direct connection to the source of all creation itself. You are a true vessel in life, up there with the likes of the great gurus, saints, and sadhus of all time. You may be celebrated or ostracised depending on the state of the world but understand that if you have been crowned and have become enlightened, it was no accident. It was meant to happen no matter the consequences, the stories of the life of Jesus Christ would be an excellent example of this. A peacemaker destroyed as a consequence of enlightenment during an age of ignorance.

When enlightened, you exist with no fear, no doubt, no hate, and no pain, and all that exists in the present moment is truth. You have access to knowledge of all that has passed and what is about to come to the present moment of life. With a heightened level of awareness and access to all knowledge, the only real challenge you may face in life would be a failure to communicate the truth to others effectively.

If you ever read the stories of Jesus's life, it was apparent that he really struggled to get his message across to the powers that be. Perhaps he knew that getting nailed to a cross would be more effective in amplifying his message than writing a book, for instance. Jesus, arguably, was also a great artist—a communicator of truth by whatever means necessary. Perhaps he foresaw the value in his crucifixion.

Solution and absolution are all you have to offer when enlightened because you recognise each creation as a sacred preserver of life. Your new role in life is to now encourage others to seek the truth for themselves and to get your message across—whether that means enlightening others with tales of truth through to retreating from society altogether or perhaps even operating as a destructive force. Your way of being may be peculiar, but you will understand your nature to be necessary.

'Blissful' is too frivolous of a word to describe this state in existence, 'neutral' would be more accurate. The world will also feel like it is in constant motion, in a constant state of creation, but you yourself will probably feel incredibly still. And though the world may very much still be in conflict, your only involvement may be to offer solutions and support those who are resolving it, and to provide absolution and support to those who seek redemption.

The clues are everywhere, the truth exists in plain sight. From the softness of the crown on a newborn baby's head through to the redemption sought by a person nearing their last breath, the truth is visible if you care to be aware. On that note, I'll share with you words that have encouraged me to continue seeking the truth for myself: do not expect to find many answers in this world, but don't stop looking for the clues. It's what my mum would say each time I picked up a book, especially religious texts and self-help manuscripts, 'Don't look for answers in any of these books, look for clues'.

IN CLOSING

A popular mystic known as Sadhguru talks of the difference between intelligence and intellect. Where intellect represents the things that we learn, intelligence represents who we are and our innate nature. Sadhguru says people should learn to 'employ intelligence without the limitations of intellect', which wonderfully reflects the value of developing your life mindfully by way of balancing your chakras, by learning from your innate intelligence.

Furthermore, Sadhguru's wisdom can also present a clue as to why you may struggle to meditate. Perhaps you are trying to meditate using your intellect when you should be employing your intelligence. Just as thinking about sleep will make sleeping difficult, thinking about meditation will make meditating difficult. You are an intelligent being, you sleep to recover from the limitations of your body, and you meditate to recover from the limitations of your mind. And if you can breathe, you can meditate.

REFERENCES

Reger MA, Stanley IH, and Joiner TE. 'Suicide Mortality and Coronavirus Disease 2019—A Perfect Storm?' *JAMA Psychiatry*. Published online (April 10, 2020). doi:10.1001/amapsychiatry.2020.1060.

Ritchie, Hannah, and Max Roser. 'Mental Health'. Published online at OurWorldInData.org (2020). Retrieved from: https://ourworldindata.org/mental-health' [Online Resource].

Ritchie, Hannah, Max Roser, and Esteban Ortiz-Ospina. 'Suicide'. Published online at OurWorldInData.org (2020). Retrieved from: https://ourworldindata.org/suicide' [Online Resource].

Shin, Jooyoung. The Physiology of Meditation. (1997). https://ejmas.com/pt/ptart_shin_0400.htm.

Sharma, Hari. 'Meditation: Process and effects'. *Ayu* (2015); 36(3), 233 – 237. https://doi.org/10.4103/0974–8520.182756.

Botvinick, Matthew, and Jonathan Cohen. 'Rubber hands "feel" touch that eyes see'. *Nature* 391, 756 (1998). https://doi.org/10.1038/35784.

Saeed SA, Cunningham K, and Bloch RM. 'Depression and Anxiety Disorders: Benefits of Exercise, Yoga, and Meditation'. *Am Fam Physician* (2019); 99 (10): 620-627.

McLeod, S. A.. 'Maslow's hierarchy of needs'. *Simply Psychology* (March 20, 2020). https://www.simplypsychology.org/maslow.html

WITH GRATITUDE

Dear reader,

Thank you for selecting and reading Meditate: Breathe into meditation and awaken your potential. This is my first book and I sincerely hope you enjoyed reading it and learning how to meditate.

I'd love to hear what you thought of it and kindly ask if you could leave a review. All your feedback will go towards improving this book and any other future projects I work on.

Thank you,

Talwinder Sidhu

PS If you would like to get in touch, work with me, or learn more about my work, let's connect!

Email: info@meditatethebook.com
Website: www.meditatethebook.com
Instagram: @meditatethebook
Facebook: @meditatethebook

Printed in Great Britain
by Amazon